The Story Of T

Book 1

Steph Young
&
Dan Mitchell

~~~

Introduction

What you are about to read in these first of two books is a narrative that I began writing in 2010 on my blog, Luminosity. The purpose of Luminosity was to tell a deeply personal story detailing a mysterious figure from my childhood that referred to itself as the "Tooth Fairy." These visits often took place in the dead of night while everyone was asleep. Being the youngest of three brothers, this entity seemed to have its focus on me but every member of my family would have strange and haunting memories from the time period of these early visitations by the "Tooth Fairy." It wasn't until many years later, probably around 2007, that I began searching for a cultural reference for this being that others could easily relate to. The experiences that I had weren't necessarily the work of aliens or ghosts, at least not that I could tell. There was something more mythical and even "elvish" about what I was witnessing that didn't fit into any specific category. For me there were poltergeist-like events, alien abduction style experiences, and powerful synchronicities that defied reason altogether. I felt it would be unfair to my own story to limit its scope to already existing narratives in the lore of the unexplained.

I would ultimately find the cultural reference I was looking for in the figure of the Harlequin. I chose that name because the entity was both clownish and acrobatic in its nature and movements. It did not fit into normal human society or human experience. It was an outlier, a misanthrope whose sudden appearances in my bedroom were inexplicable and perplexing to me even as a child. These visitations had a dream-like quality to them, while at the same time feeling hyper-realistic.

The Harlequin was a thin, androgyne being that presented itself to me at a young age, before my personality was fully-formed, when dreams and reality still occupied the same general space.   Instead of relegating those experiences to an over-active imagination, which they clearly were not, I decided to pursue their meaning.   Since my recollection of these events, which began around 1981, had been so strange and memorable, I spent over twenty-years attempting to understand what had taken place. This pursuit included talking with old friends, relatives, and other people who had figured into some of my strange memories.   This exhaustive search would take me down many dark alleys and associations with lost and unsavoury souls who were hobbling along on journeys of their own. The experience would eventually turn out to be a painful alchemical process.   I was constantly and endlessly dissolved and reified in my thinking and personal identity. By the end of it all, I had managed to decimate my own name and reputation for the sake of getting to the bottom of something that was in fact, bottomless.

I don't believe there is a concrete or scientific or psychological explanation for the things you will read here. It is very much unexplainable. The narrative is multi-dimensional and takes place in and between the seen and unseen. This book documents events that occurred between 1981 and 2007-- several years before I began writing about my experiences publicly. They are a window into many difficult years as I was grasping for answers and attempting to understand the things that plagued my mind with peculiar memories.

Steph Young has helped in this endeavour by documenting missing persons cases, paranormal encounters, and historic artifacts that correspond with the narrative contained in this book. This reveals that much of what I have written about is more common than one might expect. Steph has been a dear friend of mine for some years now and has helped me greatly in piecing parts of this narrative together with the cases she has investigated.

Dan Mitchell

I first became acquainted with Dan Mitchell when I was writing about the mysterious cases of the many young men being found dead in water across America, after going missing. Someone had suggested I take a look at his blog because he also was writing about these cases. Synchronistically, just as I was reading his blog, I received an email from Dan, and from that moment on we have developed a very close friendship. Dan's writing on the blog was exceptional and of such quality rarely seen. His intellect is incredibly sharp and his insights are astonishing. His story will shock you, terrify you, and leave you questioning everything.

Steph Young

Table of Contents

Chapter One:
Childhood Experiences

Dan Mitchell

This story begins in 1981. I was five-years-old and lived in a Polish flat with my parents and two brothers on 7th Street on the South Side of Milwaukee. My dad was born and raised in the same house by his parents, a Polish immigrant father and a German mother. It would be fair to say that there were many personal demons afoot there and many bad memories floating around in my dad's head. He was, after all, the son of an angry and sometimes abusive father.

For many people, childhood trauma is often the kick-start for anomalous events to begin. This is not a new idea, but has been covered by many writers over the years. Anne and Whitley Strieber would discuss this topic frequently in books and on podcasts bringing it to a much wider audience. This knowledge was nothing new, however. It was well-known to the ancient mind that trauma and fear often opened people up to unseen realities resulting in an ingress of unseen and subtle forces into material reality.

The initiation rites of old, which often brought people to the height of fear and closeness to death, are examples of how unseen presences might enter into ones sphere of experience. It was often through these rites that people would see their gods, demigods, heroes, and demons face to face. The face of a god or demon is never a kind or gentle face, it can be a grotesque and horrifying experience that leaves its mark upon the personality forever. Ancient rites were not just symbolic acts producing imagined fear for the sake of drama and entertainment, these rites produced literal bridges between the subtle unseen domain and the material domain. If that were not the case, these practices would have been abandoned by the ancients thousands of years ago. We know that is not the case.

In the last 60 years the closest example of an ancient rite playing out in modern culture could be a rock concert. When one watches bands like the Doors or Led Zeppelin in concert footage, the unseen energies are present and alive including in the audience. Though I don't know a great deal about rock music, I am inclined to believe that individuals like Robert Plant, Jim Morrison, and many others had experienced inexplicable paranormal events that would seem unbelievable to many of us. This may include interactions with entities not of this world. It is the emotive power in music that often pulls the individual out of the body and into places of great meaning and intensity. These same emotive powers are released with great energy in those who have experienced trauma or prolonged pain and suffering. The deaths of so many young musicians in the last three generations further exemplifies the power of these energies to profoundly damage people and turn their lives upside down. I am not saying such energies are always malignant, only that they have potential to cause great harm to the unprepared who cannot properly process these potent energies.

In 1981 I would begin to experience visitations by the Harlequin that would haunt me for years to come. It would often enter my room in the dead of night and communicate to me without words. I was never awakened by it, I always seemed to be spontaneously engaged in the communication and spontaneously wide-awake. In other words, there was never a beginning to any of these memories, just an "all-of-a-sudden." During these early visitations, the Harlequin communicated through a series of movements that I was intuitively able to understand naturally with my young mind. This was sort of the opposite of an interpretive dance. Its body was very lithe and its movements extraordinarily graceful. Not even the best dancers on earth could replicate these types of movements. The Harlequin's body would stretch and contort in ways that would cause bones to break and muscles to tear.

I struggle to remember its clothing but remember them being motley in appearance. There were strange hats and clothes that couldn't be fit into a specific period of history. The communications, from what I remember, always took the form of intuitive concepts. In alien abduction lore, this might be similar to telepathic communication. In my experience it was more complex than that. It was almost as if I was being trained to understand my existence intuitively as opposed to being immersed in the five senses and hard logic. I was being shown the subtext of reality as opposed to its physical manifestation. This would allow someone to not only grasp material reality as it appears to the senses, but to have an extended view into the unseen realm from which the material world emerges.

I do not believe that there is anything truly spectacular about this. In fact, ancient peoples viewed the world intuitively as opposed to the closed system of hard logic, reductionism, and linearity that it presently relies upon to manoeuvre through existence. It was this intuitive ability that made divine beings and sacred landscapes visible and real to people of the past. This is how their mythologies were born. It was not trial and error that gave humans the ability to know what plants could be eaten and which ones were poison. There was a time when people were still bound to a wider existence and intuitively understood what was good and healthy and what was not. By explaining this I am trying to show the reader that the life forms that inhabit the unseen are not perceived solely by the senses. They are perceived by the senses and divine intuition being united into a single entity. This is the true meaning of *Holistic*.

Intuition in the human has been atrophied nearly to the point of extinction which is why people interested in the unexplained must constantly devise various schema (logic) to understand things that precede logic to begin with and are in fact, ineffable. The ineffable can only be understood with intuitive perception. It is only when intuition and the senses are balanced that one is capable of perceiving the unseen which is already present everywhere. The Harlequin, discarnate human dead, daemons, aliens, gnomes, and all the rest live in the unseen.

I do not wish to mislead anyone. It is not merely good lifeforms that live in the unseen spectrum. There are dangerous "people" there as well. These can enter into the physical world unseen by the people they attach themselves to. They can haunt and harass folks driving people to madness and even suicide. Today this is now being mistaken as "mental illness" when in fact the root cause is spiritual.

Lacking the intuition of their ancestors, human beings today only see the physical effects of interactions between the unseen and seen. They mistakenly believe that medical intervention alone will help them against a malignant entity that has entered into their life. In our present era, there are legions of discarnate humans and other lower entities existing just slightly beyond our physical senses. They have never been able to climb the ladder out of materiality when they die because of unresolved bonds they have toward physical life. These may be traumas, fear, substance addictions, sexual addictions, and the like. Life in our present era tends to create individuals who are outward in identity; people who lack a personality that extends well beyond the temporal human identity. The more outward and selfish the person, the more chances they will become locked into their physical existence postmortem. These discarnate legions are present everywhere and their numbers grow larger every day. As the unseen legions of discarnate humans grow, so also do the number of desperate living humans who are picking up on the insanity taking place in the unseen world and being profoundly affected by it mentally.

Now the gender of the Harlequin had always vexed me. In my early childhood experiences, it was unmistakably androgyne. I viewed it either as a male or female being. Its face, nevertheless, had an ancient appearance. Its skin was pale white and sometimes appeared to be blue. On closer examination, the skin had subtle cracking as if I were looking at an old statue that had suddenly come alive. Its eyes were large and blue and their movement was always dramatic as if it were trying to be comedic. The movement of the eyes could best be described as mime-like in that they were expressive to make up for the lack of verbal communication. When it looked at me, I felt like I had absolute attention on me. This attention was so prominent that I could feel the Harlequin's attention as if it were my own. To clarify that, I was able to see these encounters as if I was slightly outside the body looking in. The most memorable physical feature were its hands. The hands looked similar to my mother's hands. It had thin fingers and somewhat bulbous knuckles on the finger joints. It perhaps sounds strange, but the hands had the appearance of ancient wisdom. It was like I was looking at the hands of a sage or individual of great knowledge. The sight of its hands always made me feel comforted as though the Harlequin had a familial relation to me. I often linked the Harlequin to my mother because she more than anyone else seemed to sense its presence. The beings mouth was always open in the shape of an "O." It never moved which solidified my belief that its face looked like a living statue. That characteristic always gave the Harlequin a look of shock and bewilderment which seemed to increase the intensity of its presence. The mouth being open in that manner made it seem as if it was trapped in a state perpetual horror, which to me contradicted the rest of its appearance.

In earlier iterations of this book, I left out an important detail. During these encounters my vision was expanded. I was able to clearly see the sign hanging on an industrial building about two-miles away from my house. On any normal evening this sign was not visible from my bedroom. This leads me to believe that I was in some kind of expanded state during the encounters. There is more. During these events the room had a blue hue that seemed to sedate my mood somewhat. This hue was similar to the way a room might look if it were bathed in the light of a full-moon. Whereas most children might scream in terror, I felt a mild sense of detachment that perhaps protected me from falling into a state of fear or shock.

In the beginning I never felt that these visitations were strange or unusual. I began asking my parents questions, though. I think it was their responses and concerns to the questions that began to make me feel otherwise about what was taking place. To my child's mind the Tooth Fairy was as real as any person. It was just a different kind of person who communicated differently. I was too young to fully grasp the division between fantasy and reality. At that age children still believe in Santa Claus and the Tooth Fairy. Like regular people it communicated and didn't show any malice initially. The familiarity I felt to it lead me to believe that maybe it was a family member that only came to visit at night while everyone slept.

Looking back on the events of my childhood, I believe the Harlequin had a familial relationship to me through the maternal side of my family. This is why its hands had the distinct appearance of the hands of members of my mom's family including myself.

A great deal of the communications I had with the Harlequin as a child felt apocalyptic in nature. It was as if it was telling me that my life was inevitably leading up to some single event of monumental importance. This importance had no real significance outside of my personal sphere. I was not chosen to carry out a particular mission to the world or to be a spokesperson for some ascended (or descended) entity. Things were never that idealistic. For me it was always a deeper personal matter. I was being pushed into these encounters to pay off some kind of karmic debt that was present in my genetic line. Many members of my family had endured some type of monumental spiritual crisis. There were energies at work in them and me that had to be worked out and processed.

It is worth mentioning that during the time of my earliest encounters with the Harlequin, my parents were devout evangelical Christians. They had spoken to us a great deal about "the last days" and approaching cataclysmic end-time events. I was immersed in these apocalyptic teachings at a young age. The apocalypse the Harlequin communicated and the "last days" my parents spoke of, were different things entirely. One followed the Christian faith of my parents, and the other seemed far less monumental but was of a more personal nature dealing with my life from beginning to end as though it were a miniature, insignificant, and separate version of the cosmos.

After moving out of our Polish flat and into a larger house in 1982, the visitations became less frequent. By that time, I had began to see the visits as increasingly strange and out of place.

Conversations I had with my parents during that time led them to believe I had an over-active imagination. However, as I would learn many years later, my mother had been experiencing some very frightening events and took my stories far more seriously than she had let on.

At that same time as the Harlequin encounters, she was having recurring nightmares of a man dressed as a woman attempting to gain entry into the house. In these nightmares the person wanted to slaughter the entire family. The most terrifying part, she explained, was that my dad would be tricked by this would-be murderer and nearly let it in the house every time. This recurring nightmare would last for months and ended only after we had moved out of the house. Her nightmare of a "transvestite" would definitely coincide with the Harlequin being an androgyne entity who was coming into the house at night. Did she sense these encounters or were these nightmares some type of screen memory that her conscious mind used to paint over things that were terrifying and unexplainable?

Around this time I remember her laying on the floor in the kitchen and in the living room with her ear pressed to the floor. Since we were living in a polish flat with the basement apartment vacant, there was no reason why anyone would be down there. My parents used that level for laundry and a small playroom for my brothers and I. She would lay there and tell us she could hear someone walking around down there. To say the least I was terrified whenever she said that. This became such an acute threat one day that she had called my dad home from work while in a panic. When he got home he searched through the basement and found it completely empty. No items were out of place and there was nothing of value missing. Yet she swears (and my oldest brother, too) that there was the sound of violent rummaging down there.

The playroom that my parents put in the basement apartment frightened me when I was young. There was a hole in the wall that my dad would always tell me to stay away from. Whenever I gazed upon it I was filled with a child's fear. For some reason I associated that hole in the wall with something dark and inexplicable as if all the bad things that happened in the house originated in that hole. I stayed as far away from it as possible. I still remember the shape of it and often wondered if my dad had experienced something on the basement level that put so great a fear into him. It was, after all, just a hole in the wall.

During the 1980s our household was devoutly Christian. There was very little talk of dreams or inexplicable events without the caveat that such discussions were possibly dangerous portals to unchristian thinking. During those years my parents ran a small house church. It was not uncommon for my father and relatives to play their guitars and sing hymns at these home services. This was all fallout from the evangelical Jesus Movement of the 1970s, which my parents and other relatives fell into. Many of the members of their house church were young and had long hair, some of them only came a few times and never returned. My brothers and I, along with the children of the adult members of the house church, would peek downstairs from the landing and laugh at the adults who sometimes seemed to be worked up into a religious frenzy while singing and playing music. Their happiness and love for Jesus brought me great comfort when I was young. However, in the end I would not follow the same path that my parents did.

Looking back to those days as a grown man with a family of my own, there were some deep-seated problems. My dad had an intimidating presence. I would often get mocked and laughed at for things I said. My mom, being deeply traditional, would stand by her husband no matter how erratic or abusive he was. This was common in conservative Christian homes, especially when churchmen used their authority as a means to prey psychologically on the members of their congregations. When I was still young, he once gave me a bath. I grew frightened after he poured a bucket of water over my head unexpectedly. When I began to scream, it sent him into a blind rage. As I tried to get out of the tub, he began to slap me across the face and throw me back into the water while yelling at me. Keep in mind that I was only four-years-old at the time. As I grew more panicked and terror-stricken, he would push me down into the water nearly drowning me. This was his attempt to "get the fear out of my heart." That is a brief snapshot from my early-life in that household. Those types of experiences, sadly, will often be foundational to the growth and development of personality as we grow older. In my case, this intimidation and abuse lead to a great deal of hostility and anger that settled into my soul at a young age.

These first traumas, I believe, were potentially the open doors through which the Harlequin entered and was able to make himself visibly appear in my life. Traumatic experiences generate intense emotive energies which reach into the unseen. When a child removes their mind from the outward world due to intense fear, they turn deeply inward which is the portal into the unseen domain. It is my opinion that introverted people are more likely to experience these types of anomalous encounters than extroverts. Introverts are often plunged into the unknown recesses of the mind space which is teeming with unseen life.

My childhood home suffered from a generational curse that repeated itself in the physical and emotional abuse of children. Since my dad despised fear, it was not something that I was ever allowed to express in a long, drawn-out sort of way. Every instance of fear was corrected by mockery and derision. Whereas parents should build up the confidence and self-esteem of their children, quite the opposite took place in our Christian home. I promised when I was still young that if I ever had children, they would never have to live in fear of me.

As contradictory as it may sound to the casual observer, my childhood was still relatively peaceful by any standard of American life in the 1980s. As overbearing as my parents could be when it came to moral and religious matters, I was blessed by the typical 80s parent neglect. I could travel freely, stay out late, and be an actual kid. I played baseball and football with my friends. I was into skateboarding. I got into a few fights and into some trouble with neighborhood parents and police. None of these things were ever all that serious. I was never sent to juvenile detention or to jail. I never got into drugs or any real trouble. Like any adolescent, I was always looking to make my mark in some way. Along with the normal events of childhood, I also continued to experience things that were not on the spectrum of normal human experience.

My childhood in the 1980s ran the gamut of strangeness. In the summer of 1984, a strange event took place in our neighborhood. I had been sitting on my porch with a friend when suddenly a huge object blocked out the sun. This cast a sudden shadow upon the entire neighborhood on an otherwise clear and sunny day. This immediately captured our attention because it was so abrupt. The object was large and structured. It appeared to be a large round disc that parked itself intentionally in front of the sun. From my perspective, it appeared to be black in color. Seeing that it had to be the size of a mountain to blot out the sun in that manner,

I began falling into a dream-like state of awe as if I was being hypnotized. Perhaps this is similar to what the lore describes as the Oz Effect. Very quickly that detached feeling of sedation came over me. I had left the world of reality and entered into something else. Reality suddenly felt fake.

After a few moments of this, I remembered seeing my friend's mom screaming and running down the street calling out her name. It felt as though all the children in the neighborhood went missing, perhaps taken into the enormous object standing in front of the sun. I watched this unfold like I was watching a movie. No way could it have been real. Numerous times before and after this event, I had been haunted by the understanding that the world I was living in was completely fake. It sometimes felt like I was on a movie set pretending that everything was real because it was compulsory to do so. This happened so many times when I was young that

I would tell people, "the world fits me loosely." Even though I would use this phrase and others similar to it, I didn't even know what it meant exactly. There was an intuitive feeling that went along with it. The phrase was more of a "feeling" that described a metaphysical state I was experiencing during those moments. In the same vein, when I was about 5 years old, my oldest brother had a VHS tape of a KISS concert. As it began, I remember feeling panicked by the appearance of Gene Simmons. I began telling my older brother, "I want to go home" to which he responded, "You are home, dummy!" Behind my words was a greater feeling, however. I knew there really was something else, not necessarily a physical place, that was home which took me away from the ugly things that scared me.

The memory of seeing the object in front of the sun has become corrupted over the years. Something from the unseen had tampered with it. The tampering began as early as the next day. While I distinctly remembered the enormous object in the sky and the parents screaming for their children, another memory seemed to be placed over it. In this false memory, everyone in our neighborhood is laughing and playing together, even the adults. A water balloon fight breaks out and there are hundreds of people in the street laughing and having a good time. The memory is not real. It feels like those corny 1980s bubble gum commercial where people are hanging out at a water park and smiling from ear-to-ear. For years I struggled with making sense of that day and knowing that I was not supposed to remember anything related to the object in the sky. At one point I became convinced that this was actually a solar eclipse and that I had somehow imagined everything. I checked to see if there were solar eclipses visible in Milwaukee in 1984. There were none.

In 2012 I contacted a friend I grew up with who had been there that day. I needed someone to corroborate these memories. To my amazement she remembered it almost as I did. She remembered seeing panicked adults scurrying about looking for their children. She also remembered it as though we were watching the events unfold from a perspective that felt outside of reality. She described it as watching a movie of the neighborhood and being in that trance-like state we enter while watching television. The only difference in our recollection was that she thought the event was a sudden bad storm that blotted out the sun and caused the neighborhood to go from a bright sunny day to instantly dark and ominous. I was so taken back by her recollection, that I began to film interviews of her speaking about her experience of that day. I found it odd that my memory was of a massive water fight and hers was of a rain storm.

A few weeks into our communication, I conveyed to her that I was possibly going to make a short documentary about the event on Luminosity. She suddenly grew frightened for her safety and that of her child. She told me that she was receiving strange phone calls in the middle of the night. It was usually an elderly-sounding man moaning her name or laughing. Her doorbell would frantically ring in the middle of the night and she was too terrified to look and see who was there. Bizarre and sometimes perverse notes were left on her car. Rather than believing this was a stalker or other deplorable, she felt my potential documentary was the sole cause of the strange happenings.

By that point she was going deep into the alien abduction lore (no thanks to me) and when night time came, those much documented stories, some true and other not so true, began to frighten her. Eventually, she demanded that I destroy the footage and notes I had taken.

During this ordeal I genuinely became frightened over my personal research. All of this was documented on Luminosity as it was happening. My personal conclusion on the matter is that going deep into the lore often causes the lore to manifest in ones personal life. I could not count how many emails I had received during the first couple years of Luminosity where people confided in me that after reading my posts that they suddenly found themselves being initiated into the same type of anomalous events. This included well-known bloggers who were writing about these topics at the time.

Like many other projects I had attempted to start something always came up to stop me from finishing. There was always something there throwing a wrench into the works. The closer I got, the further away I was. All of these things I carefully and mindfully documented on Luminosity. It was there that I wrote my deepest secrets and my most traumatic memories. I was piecing together a multi-dimensional puzzle that began a long time ago, a puzzle that I was not even sure was real.

It seemed quite telling that the story of the Harlequin would begin in 1981, the same year the phantom clown phenomenon began in Brookline, Massachusetts. Young children began telling their parents about strange clowns attempting to lure them into white vans. This would develop into a hysteria that would spread across the country, even into the Midwest where I lived. The police never had any suspects in those cases. However, the authorities once again had an explanation that everyone could live with. The phantom clowns were merely the product of children's overactive imaginations that developed into a hysteria. I never bought that. People began to forget and once again everyone could sleep better at night. To this day many believe that the phantom clowns were merely an example of the satanic panic of the 1980s.

I found the word "phantom" in these news stories very curious. It has an ephemeral sound to it. Clowns that can leap in and out of physical reality at will evading police and parents. Clowns that are bent on capturing children and taking them far away from their homes for nefarious purposes. The person that was coming into my room at night seemed able to do just that. It also was a phantom. I never saw it walk through the door; it never came in through a window. It was just there and gone whenever it wished. The encounters always lacked continuity. As I got older, the visitations changed into something more sinister. Rather than merely dancing or communicating via intuition, it started to present itself to me in ways that preyed upon my childhood fears.

The fearful part of the experience began while my family and I were sitting down to eat dinner one day. As we sat in the kitchen, I could see that my dad was agitated. I remembered it so well because I never saw him frightened and what I was witnessing was a mix of fear and agitation. Whereas my mom had been hearing things coming from the basement apartment, my dad was now aware that someone was now upstairs walking around. My bedroom, where all of these encounters were taking place, was up there. I wondered if the Tooth Fairy was looking for me. Had it somehow gotten confused by coming earlier? No matter what the reason was, the more agitated my dad got, the more the intensity of the moment began to increase to a crescendo. Within a few moments there was cacophonous laughter coming from upstairs. When I heard it, the base of my spine began to tingle and I was afraid. Looking back at this event I feel that when the laughter from upstairs began, that he also started to laugh. My dad's laughter at that moment was not a normal laughter. It was forced and born out of the terror that he was wearing on his face. There was nothing humorous in that moment to be sure.

Like other events that took place the memory essentially ends there. I came to and noticed that milk had been spilled at the table. Once it was all over everybody just went back to eating as though nothing had ever happened. This memory came up in much later conversations with both my mom and dad. My mom didn't have much to offer outside of telling me that she remembers her brother would some times stay with us and may have pulled a prank that she vaguely remembered. My dad on the other hand was disgusted entirely by any discussion related to that dinner or sinister laughter coming from upstairs.

While we were a relatively normal religious family there were always things that stood out. The house we lived in after 1982 had odd features that made little sense. In the basement of the house there was a spare bedroom with an attached bathroom. This was weird for a house that was built in 1905. Back then basements were just basements. They were not often made into liveable space. The bedroom was used by my oldest brother in the late 1980s. Before that it was used as an office by my parents.

On the stairway leading down into the basement there was a landing. On the wall at this landing there was a removable shadow board panel that would allow a person to see into the bathroom. The large mirror on the basement bathroom wall was a 2-way mirror. From the landing in the basement, one could see the entire bathroom. They would also be able to see a large portion of the bedroom if the bathroom door was left open. This means that before we purchased the house, someone had been using this feature to spy on people in the bathroom/bedroom combo in the basement. I suspect that the feature was likely installed for voyeuristic purposes by the previous owner. Even though this feature existed at the house before we moved in, it stands out as just another oddity of my childhood.

As I mentioned previously that basement room functioned as my father's office for quite some time. On numerous occasions I spotted him removing the panel to investigate the basement bathroom and bedroom. He did this at a time when nobody would have been living down there. My question was always the same. What was he expecting to see in an empty room?

We were a working poor family, but in 1985 my father purchased a video camera that in those days would have cost well over $1000. That camera was set up in his basement office on a tripod that pointed into a television screen. I would eventually find that he was recording videos of the television screen while the camera was using the same television screen as an output. This created an "infinite loop" (like having 2 mirrors facing each other) and was a form of electronic divination that he learned about. By using the camera in this manner, an electronic doorway would be created allowing one to record strange, nebulous images. Others that used this technique claimed to have filmed dead loved ones, demons, and many other inexplicable images. I saw this on a television show many years later and was mystified as to how he had heard about this. This was very difficult for me to understand given that he was an old school Christian that would have viewed such practices as satanic. It is fair to say that for a time, he became obsessed with making these videos and interpreting them by watching them in frame-by-frame in slow motion.

Those videos had strange sounds and images that I would venture to say were representative of pareidolia. I believe that he was doing this in the midst of a spiritual crisis.

He was possibly being plagued by something he didn't understand. This was likely the same process I was going through while writing Luminosity. We would have certainly been around the same age. I think that he was attempting to find evidence of something and kept his work secret from everyone.

His video camera would be a staple of my childhood. Everything we did was recorded. He had taken to filming us at family dinners, holidays, and other events. Extended family members would often yell at him to stop filming all the time. To this day I have a large library of digital copied home movies that span most of my childhood and teenage years. These videos even include the birth of my oldest children. Before he purchased the infamous video camera, he would audio record us at various times. He would ask us questions and have us answer into a microphone. The questions were mostly innocent and had to do with our thoughts on simple things like favorite foods and things we were learning about in school. On the surface it all seemed very innocuous, but deep down I feel that he was aware of something more. He was doing surveillance and didn't want to frighten anyone. This can only mean that over the years he also had been aware that something was happening in the house. I say this because many of the audio recordings have no purpose at all. They are simply left to record while everyone can be heard speaking in the distance in an entirely different room. It seemed to be some type of surveillance he was doing. Was he hoping to capture something strange? Despite him no longer being the hard-line evangelist, but a typical 80-year-old great-grandpa, he still does not wish to discuss those years but admits that strange things were taking place. I think that whatever was happening made him feel powerless, and as a man with a family there was no option to be powerless.

Quite some years ago, my dad gave me an old bible. Inside that bible was a sheet of paper that was printed on both sides and titled "Demons In The Bible". The sheet had been type-written with great care. It contained a list of nearly every bible verse that was related to demonic activity. By deduction I figured that it had been written between 1982 and 1987 in the very basement office where my dad spent his time on that typewriter. I believe even now that he knew something was happening. His only frame of reference to define it was through his Christian faith. In the end, I think his faith ultimately failed in making sense of what was happening.

In the mid-1980s my experiences became more frightening. In our neighborhood there was an ongoing rumor among the children that a strange family lived nearby. Nobody could quite say what house they lived in, but the consensus was that they lived in a rickety house on the corner of 28th and Cleveland Avenue. That house was demolished years ago to make room for an industrial building. It was the most agreed upon location of where they lived. Numerous people said they frequently saw the family's vehicle parked there. The rumor was that this family would drive around looking for young boys to kidnap and molest. Frankly, the very thought of this terrified me and other kids a great deal.

Around this time I would help an elderly neighbor named Florence take out her garbage and stop at the corner store to pick up her groceries. She usually paid me in quarters and despite the hassle she always put me through, I was always willing to help her out. One afternoon after taking out her trash, she had given me a stern warning to stay away from a particular truck that had been driving down our street more frequently. The truck had been painted in an animal print. It stuck out like a sore thumb and would always give me the creeps.

Florence proceeded to tell me that the previous night she had seen the occupants of that truck looking in the windows of her next door neighbor's house. She told me that they were interested in the little boy, Christopher, that lived there and would slow down and stare at him whenever they came down our street. She even used the word, "molest" in her warning which chilled my blood. I assured her that I would stay away from them and ran home. The entire exchange with Florence terrified me greatly. I felt like I no longer wanted to go outside.

The rumors of this strange family went on and evolved into a typical urban legend. As the story goes, another boy that I knew named Bruce had been taken by them and dropped off hours later while walking along Forest Home Ave. Everyone claimed he was never the same after that. As always, the rumors became more fanciful. Soon they were killing children in the night and the factories at the end of the block were a human slaughter operation. One day my friends and I had been playing baseball in the alley behind 28th and Arthur street in Milwaukee and saw the truck driving by slowly on 27th street. They were watching us as we could see the shadow of their heads looking toward us. We ran and hid. It was a terrible feeling to be stalked and left wondering if some monster was going to kidnap you. Real or imagined, I was scared. This felt like so much more than a mere urban legend.

The family would eventually come to be called "the inbreeds". Those that saw them up close said they didn't look quite right. Yet nobody ever knew how many were in the family. Even now I remember hanging out with groups of friends in the alley and discussing "the inbreeds" and how Bruce had now become terrified of his own shadow. While sitting together in the alley at night someone would say, "what would you do if they started driving down this alley right now?" When someone would yell, "Oh shit, there they are!" in jest I would feel a subtle paralysis of fear grip me.

Unlike most of those kids who told the more fanciful, I would end up being one of the people that actually saw them up close and personal. Looking back on that day over thirty-seven years ago, I still remember the fear it invoked. I remember the abstract yet very real people I saw in the truck that day.

In the winter of 1986 there was a terrible accident on nearby 27th street, which was a busy thoroughfare. The traffic was being re-routed down the street I lived on. I remember that it was winter and I was playing on snow drifts alongside the street when I saw the animal patterned truck in the distance. For reasons I do not know, I decided to wait and see the occupants of the truck for myself. I was relatively close to my house and likely felt that if I had to run I could make it to my house. I felt frozen by fear and anticipation, but even if I wanted to run away, I would not have been able to. I was stuck like a magnet and the truck was getting closer. I could feel my heart pounding out of my chest. Would I be taken? Would I see something that I did not want to see? I remembered Florence's warning to keep away, but I simply could not move. The only positive thing I remembered thinking was that it was still a bit light outside. Somehow I felt that this would thwart them from trying to take me.

As they got closer, I was able to make out distinct shapes through the wind shield. There were three or maybe four of them inside. Their eyes were fixated upon me and nothing else. I could see their eyes and was awash in fear. Standing upon the snow drift I was at a slightly higher elevation than they were. I was looking down at them slightly. As we crossed paths my mind began to race. I struggled to hold what I was seeing. Their faces clearly weren't right. One of them seemed to be missing its lower jaw completely. I could only make out its upper teeth and huge eyes. Everything I saw in that truck could be summarized as eyeballs and abstract human-like shapes. It was terrifying. My mind could not make out or put together what I was looking at. The eyeballs were fixated on me, but no matter how hard I tried, I could not piece any shape inside the truck into a coherent human form, only eyeballs, noses, teeth, and stringy hair in a chaotic mix.

As the truck passed and our gazes broke, the fear paralysis let up and I ran inside the house. I would tell this story to friends which simply enforced the ever-continuing saga of "the inbreeds". Even years after this event, including once as an older teenager, I would see the truck roaming along on the south side of

Milwaukee from time to time. As I got older, the fear of it faded away but the strange feeling it gave me remains. I have noticed a recurring phenomenon of events like this; my memories of these encounters always feel tampered with. I am left wondering if what I saw was flavored by fear, or if my memory is true and the images I saw in the cab of that truck represented something truly horrifying and dangerous.

During this same period other things were happening as well. Our family owned a cottage in the north woods near Eagle River, Wisconsin. The cottage was quite isolated and sat on thirty-three acres of land directly on Black Oak Lake. It was like paradise going there as a child. I was free to roam the property, shoot guns, start large controlled fires, fish, and sit out under the stars late into the evening. We always went up in late August when vacationers were largely headed home. This let us have the lake mostly to ourselves for fishing and boating. In the evenings we would go into town for ice cream. The roads to and from the cottage were mostly gravel and there were no street lights. So walking out there without a flash light at night was impossible. My dad would often drive fast down these gravel roads and turn off the headlights to scare us. He knew the roads so well that he felt it would be a relatively safe way to scare us. The feeling of moving very quickly while being unable to see your hand in front of your face was terrifying.

One evening while driving on the roads and turning off the headlights, my mom noticed movement ahead of us. When my dad turned the lights on, he illuminated a strange looking man pushing a stroller down the gravel road. Everybody in the car became dead silent with fear. It was as if there was a silent gasp. I had been out on those roads at night with a flash light and knew there was no way anyone could walk without a light. Being as isolated as we were, to see anybody that late in the evening was very odd. That this person was pushing a stroller and didn't have a flash light terrified everyone. The rest of the drive was quiet. I remember wanting to pack up and go home that same night. I was terrified of this man walking toward our cottage or staring in the windows while we slept. The thought of that haunted me to no end. As usual I could not make out the face as we passed by him. It seemed obscured. It was hidden behind the ambiguity typical of these types of events. Luckily we had never laid eyes on this man and his stroller again. Another story for the annals.

Throughout the latter part of the 1980s I began to suffer from a terrible fear that I was going to be kidnapped. I remember walking to school and constantly looking over my shoulder. I had a recurring dream that I was taken by a man in a white Volkswagen beetle who would keep me in a large wooden box with two eye holes cut into it. Deep down I knew that I was going to be trapped in that box forever. Such nightmares were common. My mind was preoccupied with dark thoughts that I could not escape. It was as if an unseen presence was always nearby presenting itself to me through diverse manifestations of thought and phantom phenomena like the Harlequin.

Around this same time, I became convinced that there was a secret room in our house that could be accessed through a small wine cellar in the basement. There was a space behind that wall that seemed to be the size of a large walk-in closet. I told my cousin this belief and she thought I was crazy. After moving several large carboys from the corner of the cellar, there was a hole in the wall at about knee level. I crouched down and looked in and to my amazement began seeing shapes. The objects seemed to be made of static. There was no color, just black and white as if one was looking into a dimly lit room. Soon the shapes began to come together into a tangible form.

Through the hole I saw a figure sitting on a chair. The closer I looked, the more the sight forming in front of me seemed cartoonish. The shape was muppet-like in appearance staring back at me. It looked similar to Oscar the Grouch but with a far meaner and more ominous look to it. The manner in which it stared back at me communicated that it wanted to harm me. I began to feel threatened as its face looked angered and ready to bite. I instantly felt an explosion go off in my head which caused me to jump back and run out of the cellar with my cousin. I was fighting back tears. I did not want to tell my parents about this because I knew how they would respond with anger and disbelief. The experience itself was reminiscent of a fever dream a child might have.

Just like the two-way mirror set-up at the landing of the basement stairs, I believe there was indeed a space behind the wall in the cellar. If I were to guess it was a false wall the previous owners installed. Thinking about this now I wonder if the previous owners were running some kind of illegal operation out of the house that required these features to be installed. The previous owners of the house made updates that were suspicious. I was with my parents at the closing on that house. I remember the previous owners being with us in an office. It was a husband and wife. Did they disclose these strange features of the house? My dad seemed to be aware of them early on.

Anecdotal experiences like sinister muppets hiding in secret rooms became normal happenings for me. So many of these memories have a nightmarish quality. I often questioned whether I was losing my mind. I concluded early on that things were not what they appeared to be. There was far more complexity to these encounters than the simple answer of mental illness or an over-active imagination.

Even though I had partially dismissed the Harlequin visitations as childhood imagination as I got older, the peculiar memories and inner states never left me. The early visitations always remained as the source point of every other odd event that occurred. I saw all of them as related, a meta-phenomenon that stretched through the years. The Harlequin seemed to be the personification of all of it, the image from which all other events I was exposed to emerged.

One thing was certain, the anomalous experiences I was having were constantly changing. They were always developing and evolving as I grew older and matured. They often came forth as custom made for maximum shock value to my soul. I came to believe that whatever was causing them knew my deepest, darkest fears and was able to exploit them at will by presenting them to my conscious mind. The question I could not answer was if the experiences were meant to somehow help me in an indirect way or harm me? I simply did not know.

It was not until I became an adult that I began to realize that whatever was causing these things to happen belonged to a reality that was in some way attached to my sleeping, unconscious mind and my genetic history. As the phenomenon developed, it seemed to follow my interests and my understanding of the world. It interjected itself wherever and whenever it could. I would learn that the more attention I gave to it, the stronger it would become.

Chapter Two:
The Harlequin & Mr. Punch

Steph Young

In the Arts, the Harlequin originates from the 16th Century Italian Mask plays the 'Commedia dell'arte all improviso,' or 'the comedy of the arts of Improvisation.' The first recorded performances were in Rome in 1551 and performed by professional actors in outdoors temporary venues. The actors were dressed in costumes and wore masks. Pantomime, which began in the 18th century, was inspired by the Commedia dell'arte, and in particular by the character of the harlequin.

The most well-known characters of the Commedia are the Harlequin, also known as 'Arrlechino', Columbine, the servant girl he loves, Pantaloon, Columbine's father, and Pierot. There is also the character of Punch, or 'Pulcinella,' from which the Punch and Judy shows were inspired. There is the 'Harlequinade' too, which is a British comic theatrical genre.

'Arlecchino,' or 'Harlequin' wore a motely costume of tight-fitting long jacket and matching trousers with uneven shaped patches, usually in the colours of green, yellow, brown and red. The Harlequin is characterized now by his chequered, brightly-coloured diamond-shaped patches, his spangled tights and his mask. Originally though, he wore a multi-coloured patchwork tattered outfit which bore resemblance to a wild-man, or perhaps we could say a hobo, then this later morphed into the more refined and cultured tight-fitting bodices tunics and tights.

Originally, the Herlequin's face was covered with a black half-mask. Sometimes he wore a black stocking wound around the lower part of his face and then up over his head. He had once been hirsute though – early depictions show his face covered in thick dark hair, giving him the appearance of a feral creature from the forest. He wore a hat with either a rabbit or fox's tail, but now he wears what is more like a Jester's hat, and usually he wears a red or black mask.

On stage he was a nimble, almost death-defying acrobat, whose stunts astounded and thrilled the audience. His character was that of a sharp, astute, but light-hearted servant, often intent on thwarting the plans of his master and others with cunning wit, resourcefulness, and his trickster qualities. He would have a direct interaction with the audience, involving them in his plans through gestures. His behaviour is inherited or inspired from the character of a mischievous devil in the older mediaeval passion plays. He tries to trick his masters, through plotting, but his plans would not usually work despite this. He carries a wand which is capable of magic.

He loves Columbine, who is a comic but cunning servant girl. She is sometimes

Harlequin's mistress, or rather, the one he loves but cannot have because she is also the wife of Pierrot. Columbine appears in a raggedy patch-work dress and heavy face paint. She appears without a mask but she uses several disguises to trick and confuse both Harlequin and the audience. Her father Pantaloon, tries his best to separate Harlequin and Columbine, in league with the mischievous Clown and the servant Pierrot. The acts of this cast of characters are all carried out through mime and music.

The Harlequin character first appeared in Europe in the 17th century as centre stage of the Harlequinade, that part of Pantomime where the harlequin and clown play the principal parts for an extended comic scene to the thrill of the audience, and in modern day it is the part of the pantomime where the audience shouts out at them, although rarely now is a Harlequin seen, just the clown instead.

The Harlequin in contrast to the clown was more sophisticated and refined. The Harlequin was attributed with the ability to do magic. The French Harlequin could turn himself into different people. The English Harlequin of early pantomime could transform the things around him by hitting them with his magic wand or bat. In early versions, his wand or staff had two entwined serpents. His staff, since antiquity representing the phallus, makes the Harlequin openly sexual and satyr-like. He is also a chameleon by nature, as visualized in his various costumes. He is a trickster, and the word 'harlequined' means to conjure away as if by a harlequin's trick. He likes to instigate chaos.

The first known appearance of the Harlequin on stage was in 1262, when the character of a masked and hooded devil appeared in 'Jeu da la Feuilliere,' a play by Adam de la Hall. In fact, a number of harlequins appear, playing the roles of intermediaries of King Hellekin, the prince of

Fairyland. In French, the Harlequin was a spirit of the Air, with his ability to ride the night sky, and become invisible.

As to the origins of the Harlequin, views are divided. Historian Otto Driesen suggested that the Harlequin derived from the Mediaeval French daemon 'Herlequin.' Driesen traced the Harlequin to 'Harlekin' (variations of the name also being Herlekin and Hellequin) to literature from 1100, in which the Harlequin is a ragamuffin of demonic visage and appearance as well as character. Harlequin may also derive from the Italian figure of 'Zanni' – the village idiot, the stock servant comic buffoon, but 'Zanni' was also a creepy, treacherous trickster character of the Commedia, with his hideous and frighteningly extreme pointed long-nosed mask, and he was a keeper of dead people's souls.

In Dante's 14th century 'Inferno,' there is a devil by the name of 'Alichino,' the other name for the harlequin. It was believed that the Devil was so wicked and so feared that he required a mask to cover his face from the audience and that no human's face could resemble such hideousness behind the mask.

There is an old French term 'Herlequin hellequin,' as written in the chronicles of 11th century Benedictine monk Orderic Vitalis. Vitalis writes of the case of a monk called Walkelin in 1091, who was pursued by a dancing troop of demons when he was traveling the coastline of Normandy one night. The troop of demons were led by a masked club-wielding giant known as 'familia harlequin.' The monk watched as hundreds charged past him; men, women and children, animals, god-fearing men and priests, Knights and dwarfs with huge heads, demons, neighbours; all charged past him. He recognized many of them as deceased neighbours, dead since many years ago.

The women were riding side-saddle on huge black horses, their saddles "marked with red hot nails." As they rode, the power of the wind would pull them from their saddles up into the air, and they would land back on the nails in their saddle, leaving them stabbed and bleeding. Writes Vitalis: "All lamented bitterly, bewailing the torments they suffered." An enormous tree-trunk was being carried by two men, on which was strapped and bound "some wretch tightly trussed, suffering tortures." A fearful demon was sitting astride the same tree trunk. The demon was sticking "red-hot spurs" into the man's loins.

Walchelin was convinced he was watching an army of dead pass by. "This was undoubtedly the Hellequin's Army, doomed souls marching through the land. It had been a folktale for many years. Now I do indeed see the shades of the dead with my own eyes." This story, of the Mesnee d'Hellequin, appears to be a medieval version of the Germanic Wild Hunt, with the

Herlequin as the figure of Herla cyning, the 'host king.'

In Germanic Paganism, the Harii, led by the Harlequin, fought at night taking the appearance of an army of ghosts. The harlequin is the leader of the involuntary dead, in a parallel with Odin. The Harlequin is depicted as a black-faced emissary of the Devil. He roams the countryside in the dark of night with his band of demons, seeking the souls of evil persons to carry them to Hell. They ride across the sky on the back of giant black horses or black goats, huge hounds baying alongside them. Those who hear the approaching din must not look for they risk being dragged into the procession of the dead. Practitioners of various forms of magic were believed to join in, voluntarily, though not necessarily physically joining the procession, but rather, working remotely.

Hellequin is also thought to be related to the Old English Herla, a character often identified with Woden, the lord of magic, the shaman, and the leader of the Wild Hunt. In 1127 a new Abbot, Henry of Poitou, arrived at Peterborough Abbey. The Anglo-Saxon Chronicle says: 'Immediately after his arrival many men both saw and heard a great number of huntsmen hunting. The huntsmen were black, huge and hideous, and rode on black horses and he-goats...and their hounds were jet-black with eyes like saucers and hideous....'

Now we come to Mr. Punch, a character derived from the Harlequin. A puppeteer called Signor Bologna came from Italy with a marionette of Pulcinella to perform in London. Eventually, as he travelled through Europe, this marionette puppet became known as Punch. Somewhere around 1800 he became a hand puppet. The other Commedia characters came with Punchinello. The clown Scaramouche, would eventually become one of Punch's victims. It had been the Harlequin who carried the cudgel in the Commedia, but Punch took it from him when they came to England.

Punch, shortened from 'Punchinello' was the most popular of the Puppets or Marionettes. Again, of Italian origin but the history of this figure and his name is shrouded in obscurity. Punch has a ruddy complexion, with big rosy cheeks painted on his wooden face, and his expression is fixed in a wide perpetual grin. His red lips and mouth are huge, his nose is huge and red and hooked. He has big staring blue or green eyes.

'Pulcinella' is a maverick, a subversive, defiant, and an anarchist. He is a virulent and violent character and yet comical too. Wouldn't we all want to be Punch at some level? He is a rascal but an "Everyman." For all the husbands of "nagging wives," for all the youths who would flout authority, for the workers of the daily grind, he represents joyous anarchy and purposeful rebellion with abandon to consequences. He was also, for a child, quite disturbing to watch too; his menace, his physicality, his unpredictability, his aggression.

According to the 1911 Encyclopædia Britannica, early etymologists sought to trace the name of 'Punchinello' to various mythical individuals. There was Puccio d'Aniello, a wine maker from Naples who, with a "grotesque appearance" was induced to join the troop and whose place after death was taken by a masked actor who imitated his dress and manner. By far the most mysterious is the theory given by Encyclopædia Britannica, with the name of Punch cryptically deriving 'from some old mystery representing Pontius Pilate and Judas, or the Jews,' and describing this theory as 'formerly popular.' The mystery itself is not stated however.

From childhood, for me, watching many Punch and Judy shows at the seaside in Dorset, England, he was a fun fantasy character, who's thrill came from his answer to authority: he would beat everyone with a stick. In this pantomime, his arch nemesis was a crocodile, who would steal his string of sausages, but his ever-handy baton would be used to beat his nagging wife savagely and the policeman too, in front of us spectators.

His violence was certainly extreme but accepted until political correctness set in. It was a joke, a game, a pantomime, not real. It was outrageous, slapstick, an escape, and it was the staple of Englishness at the Seaside. Other characters apart from Judy his wife and their baby, include his dog Toby, Scaramouch the neighbour - a figure with an extending neck, Hector a hobbyhorse, the Blind Man, Joey the Clown, the Policeman, a Quack Doctor, the Crocodile, Sweet Polly the Mistress, The Ghost, The Hangman, and The Devil. The Ghost is only occasionally seen now. The Devil, who was once a central character is now only rarely seen too, the Crocodile having taken the Devil's place.

Mr. Punch may beat his adversaries, even those closest to him, including beating his own baby to death in frequent scenes, but his 'victory' comes most when he defeats the very Devil himself. On watching a performance, Punch is depicted as a sadistic bully, who operates on the lowest common denominator – that by pure brutality he can inflict pain and suffering upon all his foes, on anyone who crosses him, or rather, who order him about, and yet, when we look at his enemies perhaps it is they who are the bullies – the bossy domineering wife, the authority figure of the Beadle, representing bureaucracy and the petty civilian rules of society, the criminal justice figures of the Policeman and the hangman; and finally, the supernatural terror of the dreaded appearance of the Devil.

So, perhaps most of us could possibly say, he is the victim and righteously standing up for himself. (Apart from killing his screaming baby, of course) A typical plot would be as such: When the baby won't stop crying, he throws it out the window. His wife Judy, understandably horrified and outraged gets a cudgel to teach Punch a lesson. He wrestles the cudgel from her, and after a ferocious beating, Judy is dead and is then also thrown out of the window. Punch says his catchphrase, "That's the way to do it," whenever his violence bears fruition.

A policeman soon arrives on the scene, no doubt alerted by bystanders who have heard the shouting and screaming and commotion. He too lasts a very short time, as Punch dispatches him also, with a savage beating. Next to arrive will be a doctor, a blind man, a 'foreigner,' or crocodile! (who is after Mr Punch's string of sausages) followed shortly after by the hangman. All are to find themselves besieged by a short-fused and impulsive Punch, who cares only to deal with them in the most primitive way – with brute force and violence. Finally, and particularly in the earlier plays, the devil himself appears, but even he is fought with and beaten by Punch.

Punch has duality – he is variably both servant and master. As servant, Encyclopædia Britannica describe him as a coarse dullard and bumpkin. As master, it describes him as a 'proud, cunning, scheming' figure, with great intellect and 'aggressive sensuality.' Punch either plays dumb but knows very much what is going on, or he acts as though he is the most intelligent and competent of all the characters, though he can be joyfully and woefully ignorant too. He is a chameleon. The British Punch is far more fun and child-like than his Italian counterpart, but also much more violent and sharply menacing.

The independent website 'punchandjudy.com,' a resource for all things related, says; 'Before the curtain rises everybody knows that he is about to commit more murders than Bluebeard and are delighted at the prospect of watching him do them,' and adds: 'What about justice? Nobody cares tuppence for justice. When the strong arm of the law is dealt with everybody laughs, and Punch hangs the hangman in his own noose. Everybody cheers.'

Rosalind Crone, in 'Mr. & Mrs. Punch in 19th Century England' suggests that, as the puppets are carved from wood, their facial expressions cannot change, but are stuck in the same exaggerated pose, which, in her interpretation helps to deter any sense of realism and to distance the audience; but couldn't it also be said that, rather more disturbingly, it succeeds most in heightening the sense of the macabre, the grotesque and the horrifying, for anyone who has a nervous disposition when it comes to seeing clowns and similar such characters come-to-life.

The fixed wide gaping grin of Mr. Punch, combined with his huge, hooked blood-red nose and bulging eyes could indeed be a face to haunt one's dreams at night, particularly if troubled by such a condition as Coulrophobia, or fear of clowns. His exaggerated facial features and body parts, deformed and monstrous, transforms him into the 'evil clown', the monster in the closet and other such archetypal creatures from our darkest dreams, or perhaps even our reality, such as in Dan's case with his very real visitations from the Harlequin. Clowns, jesters, tricksters, jokers and harlequins have appeared for centuries throughout many cultures; the court jesters of medieval England, Pygmy clowns of ancient Egypt, and Ancient Rome's the stupidus figure.

The Smithsonian quotes French literary critic Edmond de Goncourt, who wrote in 1876, "The clown's art is now rather terrifying and full of anxiety and apprehension. Their suicidal feats, their monstrous gesticulations and frenzied mimicry reminding one of a lunatic asylum."

The less manic clowns, the staple troubled, sad, and tragic clown variety in the form of the tattered "hobo" homeless clowns were no less troubling to watch. There are some horrifying claims, though not easily substantiated, that in the Middle Ages, jesters were mutilated if they failed to make the court laugh; their faces cut into a permanent smile by the removal of their muscles that would make frowns.

As for the release of the 2017 Stephen King movie 'IT,' his clown is now depicted in classic Harlequin quality, with elegance of costume. 'Pennywise' has been described by theatre critics as 'a harlequin-from-hell.' Of course, in the fore-front of people's psyche will always be John Wayne Gacy's clown Pogo. Between 1972 and 1978 he sexually assaulted and killed more than 35 adolescent boys. When he went to entertain children and adolescents, dressed in his clown costume, what no-one knew was that he had already been convicted of sexually assaulting a teenage boy.

In contemporary times, Stephen King's demon clown 'Pennywise,' Heath Ledger's 'The Joker' in Batman and also 'Punch and Judy' as the henchmen of the Joker, DC Comics' cloddish supervillains 'Punch and Jewellee,' and perhaps even the Insane Clown Posse's grease-paint and their Dark Carnival performances, have all only solidified the fear of the unpredictable often frenzied persona of the murderous Clown or any other similar trickster characters, and this abiding fear lies in the soul of not just children but us adults too.

In the 'Clown sightings' outbreak of 2016 throughout America and England, online magazine Mashable synchronistically remarked; 'Since the late summer, there have been about a half-dozen reports of clown sightings. Alleged sightings mapped along the border between the

Carolinas, form a sort of 'harlequin triangle' between Greenville, Greensboro and Winston – Salem, North Carolina.'

The Washington post pointed out: 'The incident seems to follow a script that has repeated itself several times over in the area since late August: Witnesses phone local police to report a menacing clown or clowns, but officers cannot verify the sightings.'

Fortean Loren Coleman first used the term "Phantom Clowns" after researching a "clown flap" in the early 1980's, of children possibly being bundled into run-down and archaic vans. Patrick Harpur in Daimonic Reality wrote of a strange and troubling variation: heavily made up "Phantom Social Workers." In the early months of 1990 across England a similar pattern to the "Phantom Clowns" played out. Instead of clown costumes, they came wearing suits and heavy make-up on their faces. The police dealt with an ever-growing number of reports from concerned and distressed parents who had received unexpected visits from social workers who had turned up on their doorsteps, asking to come in to see their children. When the parents became suspicious, they would retreat and leave. Mostly these visitors were women, wearing very heavy make-up that would have been wholly inappropriate for a social worker.

They carried identification and clip boards. Sometimes they did phone in advance. "Operation Childcare" was set up by combined police forces to track down these bogus authority figures. Sometimes they were reported to operate in groups but strangely the police felt it was several different groups. Were they real paedophile groups, phantoms, or like the so-called Men In Black visits?

Fear of clowns and similar such disturbing characters is attributed by some to the "uncanny valley effect." This is said to be the phenomenon where things that look human but aren't quite, are as a result, deeply unsettling to the human psyche. Our reaction upon seeing such grotesque monsters is a dip in emotional response that occurs as we are confronted by such. The term "uncanny valley" derives from robot maker Masahiro Mori, in 1970, who hypothesised that as robots grew more human in appearance and character, people would grow to accept them as more familiar when compared to earlier more mechanical and rudimentary models. However, the closer they became to human-like, the more disconcerted and uncomfortable people became and their responses of unease heightened.

Exaggerated postures and exaggerated facial features on human-like faces unsettle our subconscious, unnerve us with their unpredictability, and threaten us. Perhaps the greatest fear from all of these archetypes is that their unnaturally fixed exaggerated and grotesquely frozen expressions make them so surreal, so nightmarish, and that these faces seem to hide their real nature... When the grease-paint is wiped off, what is left....?

As to the Harlequin, on reading an account of Dan's visitation on Jason Offutt's blog where it first appeared, a reader called Kevin contacted Offutt. He believed he had once been visited by a Harlequin. He said: 'I remember lying in bed. I could hear the jingle jingle of a bell coming closer. That's when I see the harlequin come into my room. The Harlequin is dancing....I can hear what sounds like two knives scraping together. I see blades at the end of its fingers as it dances around....I remember the smell of summer rain ... and I could also hear faint giggling...."

Another reader commented: 'I remember having conversations with what looked like Mr. Punch in my bedroom when a kid. He used to whisper disturbing secrets to me till I screamed, after which he would become sad and a bit angry and leave." On reddit a writer describes: 'As a kid about 7 years old, the window curtains flew open and what I can only describe as a cross between Maleficient and a harlequin popped her (its?) head inside and screamed at me. It felt very primal, kinda of like a SHUT-UP type of scream. As if it was trying to drown out my crying. It never took its eyes off me. I was so shocked, I just sat there staring at it and then it left. My grandpa came back but I didn't tell him about what I saw. I went to the backyard and looked everywhere, but I couldn't find any trace of this figure. I've only seen it once, but I have heard stories from my mom and aunts and uncles about my grandparents' house, about how they all saw something really weird there before.'

But for Dan, his Harlequin did not look like Mr Punch. It was, as he says, 'Very lithe and its movements extraordinarily graceful, unmistakably androgynous. Its face made it look very old.   Its eyes were very large and blue.' This called to mind an old account I once read.   Maurice   Henry   Hewlett,   an   English Barrister, historian and essayist in the 1800's, and an experiencer of unnatural entities, wrote Lore of Posperine, in which is an account of the strangest of creatures and the sinister results of its appearance.

'The facts were as follows. A Mr. Stephen Mortimer Beckwith, 28, clerk in the Wiltshire & Dorset Bank at Salisbury was living in Wishford. He was married with one child. At approximately 10 pm on the 30th November 1887, he was going home after spending the evening at a friend's house. It was a mild night, with rain and a wind was blowing. There was a quarter moon and it was not completely dark. Accompanied by his dog, he was riding a bicycle. He stated that he had no difficulty seeing the road nor the stones on it nor the sheep in the hillside. He recalled quite clearly seeing an owl flying.'

'A mile or so along and his terrier dog ran through the hedge and ran barking up the hill. The man imagined he was after a hare and called him, but the dog took no notice and ran to a gorse bush then stopped, paw uplifted and watching it intensely.'

The man watched his dog for some minutes, dismounting from his bicycle. He could see nothing up there himself but the dog was in a state of excitement. It was whimpering and trembling, and his master decided to take a look at what was causing this behaviour in his dog, 'Strap.' The dog would not take his eyes off whatever was up there.

The man finds something in the bushes: 'No movement of the features could be discerned. The face was very small -- about as big as a big wax doll's," and "of a longish oval, very pale." He adds, "I could see its neck now, no thicker than my wrist; It had not the size of what we call a girl, nor the face of what we mean by a child."

He could see "the clear grey of its intensely watchful eyes. It was, in fact, neither fish, flesh, nor fowl. Strap had known that from the beginning, and now I was of Strap's opinion myself."

She was "most curiously dressed in a frock…of stuff like cobweb." He could not recognise the material. When he found her in the gorse bush, she'd had a "gaping wound" on her long neck. He had bound his handkerchief around her neck to stop the blood – and yet, he didn't see any blood, and later, when he took off the handkerchief, "there was no blood upon it."

When he takes her home to his wife, his wife is standing on the front doorstep, waiting for him, wondering why he is so late home. He begins to explain his lateness, and as he does so, his wife reaches her arm out to lean on the bicycle. The 'girl' is sitting on his bicycle, but his wife's arm passes clean through her, and his wife cannot see her.

Only his small daughter can see the 'girl,' too, but this would lead to tragedy. The 'girl' was placed in the dog kennel outside. He gave her the name 'Thumbeline.' His little daughter would go out and play with her. It went on for months. His wife had no idea.

When playing with his daughter and his two small dogs, the girl/creature is described as "incredibly graceful.... circling... weaving her arms, pointing her toes, arching her graceful neck, inviting .... darting away like a Fairy at her magic. You couldn't hear the fall of her foot."

Then came the terrible day. "I blame myself for it...." the bank clerk writes, "My full confession I have made to my wife, the police, the newspapers. On the 13th May, Thumbeline and our only child disappeared... I had left them in the meadow... Thumbeline had been crowning

Florrie with a wreath for flowers... I don't doubt now she was bewitching Florrie...."

"My wife found a few picked wild flowers but no other traces. There were no footprints in the mud.... we explored every fold of the hills, every hedgerow... we found no trace of our dear one... We might have been spared if, on the night I brought her home, I had told my wife the whole truth. And yet, how could I? Is not that an absurdity? Yes, but the sequel was no absurdity."

His daughter was never seen again.

This is just one possible tale of a missing child and a 'trickster.' There is also the story of the Pied Piper. The legend of the Pied Piper dates back to the Middle Ages, with the earliest references describing a piper, dressed in multi-colored clothing. In fact, "pied" means 'having two or more different colours,' or motley, as was his dress, and just like the Harlequin.

'The strangest figure! His queer long coat from heel to head was half of yellow and half of red, And he himself was tall and thin, with sharp blue eyes, each like a pin, No tuft on cheek nor beard on chin, But lips where smile went out and in; There was no guessing his kith and kin: A scarf of red and yellow stripe, To match with his coat of the self-same cheque.'

This was poet Robert Browning's description of 'The Pied Piper of Hamelin.' It was a story told to children as a 'Fairy Tale,' but, this tale is in actual fact, based on a true event. It took place in the small rural town of Brunswick, in the county of Hamelin, near Hanover in Germany. The year was 1284 A.D. and the event was recorded in the official town records, and later memorialized in a stained-glass window of the Church there, dated to the year 300 A.D. The Church and the window that displayed its record of the missing children was destroyed in a blaze in 1660, but a number of written accounts held in other places have survived. The mountain where the children disappeared is called Poppenberg, a tree-covered mountain within the Harz National Park.

'As they reached the mountain-side, A wondrous portal opened wide, As if a cavern was suddenly hollowed; And the Piper advanced and the children followed, And when all were in to the very last, The door in the mountain-side shut fast.'

The story goes that in the town, a plague of rats descended. They ate their way through all the stores of food, and bit people while they slept, and generally terrified everyone. With their food supplies rapidly disappearing and the officials running out of ideas about how to drive the rats out of town, they held an emergency meeting.

As the councillors debated what they could do, there was a knock on the meeting-room door. The Mayor instructed the person on the other side of the door to enter, and, as the poem describes, in came a rather mysterious person.

'In did come the strangest figure! A wandering fellow with a gipsy coat of red and yellow. And he himself was tall and thin. Lips where smiles went out and in. There was no guessing his kith and kin!'

Curiously, another of the councillors adds; "It's as if my great-grandsire, starting up at the Trump of Doom's tone, Had walked this way from his painted tomb!" In other words, he looks like a walking cadaver. The oddly dressed 'man,' wearing motley and garish clothing yet looking like the walking-dead, tells them that for a price, he is able to solve their problem. "I'm able, by means of a secret charm, to draw All creatures beneath the sun after me. And I chiefly use my charm..... people call me the Pied Piper."

"Into the street the Piper stept, smiling first a little smile, as if he knew what magic slept in his quiet pipe; From street to street he piped advancing, and step for step they (the rats) followed dancing.'

With his magickal pipe, the rats ran behind him as he played his beguiling tune, and as he got to the River, they threw themselves in and drowned. The rats were driven out of the village; however, the Piper had named his price for the job and it was exceptionally high. The Major, in his desperation to save the village from the rats, had exclaimed it was too much, but had agreed to pay it. However, now the rats had left, the Major reneged on his deal. The Mayor instead now offers him only a trifle of the sum, and the mysterious, strangely-dressed cadaver-like figure, is not happy. He tells the Mayor, "Folks who put me in a passion may find me pipe to another fashion."

It is a very dangerous threat, and yet the Mayor does not understand what he means by it; until the Piper demonstrates it, by carrying out the threat. He plays his pipe once more, only this time, it is not rats that follow him; it's the village children, following him blindly just like the rats. The children follow him unfalteringly, seemingly without any ability to resist. Forming a long procession behind the bright coat-tails of the Piper, he leads them out of the village and into the forest.

The Mayor, his officials, and all the parents seem unable to physically move to try to stop them. It is as if they are all frozen to the spot. As the children reach the mountainside, "A wondrous portal opened wide, As if a cavern was suddenly hollowed."

In went the Piper, followed by all of the children, and they were never seen again. Many written historical accounts which came after the event appear to back the story up.

Possibly the earliest known written record is that which is found in the Decan Lude of Hamelin's Chorus Book, written in the late 1380's, which held a written account in Latin by an eye-witness to the event. Then there is the Lueneburg Manuscript from the 1440's in which it states; 'In 1284, on June 26, by a piper clothed in many colors, 130 children were seduced and lost near the hillside.'

In 1556, J. Fincelius' De Miraculis sui Temporis (translated as 'The Miracles of Time') also describes the story and determines that the Piper is the Devil. The story itself has remained the same ever since it happened, but there are alternative views as to what really did happen to the children. There are no doubts in any of the records that the children, en-masse, did indeed disappear. One theory is that the children were victim to the Black Plague; and yet the plague would have killed old and young, not just the children. Additionally, the most prevalent time of the Black Plague in Europe was in the 1350's, more than fifty years after the mysterious event occurred. Another theory suggests that the children were taken to fight as child soldiers in the Crusades, although the Crusades were not taking place in Germany.

Robert Burton's The Anatomy of Melancholy of 1621, depicts the Piper figure as a supernatural entity, again as the Devil; 'In likeness of a Piper, the devil carried away the children that were never seen after.'

Was he the devil, or an archetypal Trickster figure, with his strange and garish clothing? Was he an adept at magic instead, and possessed of the ability to charm the children, 'seducing' them with the unseen allure of his mystical powers? But why did he look dead...?

Chapter Three:
"We Are Coming Through The Walls"

Dan Mitchell

From 1989 to 1993 the strange experiences began to taper off to some extent. The experiences I did have always revolved around seeing UFOs and the feelings and states they induced in me. These experiences include very brief memories, literally fractions of a second, of lights coming in through my bedroom windows and paralysis. Looking back at those years it seems obvious why very few events manifested. Since I was going through puberty, and constantly changing in both body and mind, the strangeness potentially had no clear way to manifest itself. I was too preoccupied with other things to focus on things that went deep. Therefore, the strangeness remained in the shadows for years waiting for an opportunity to reveal itself again.

This all changed in the summer of 1993. I had fallen asleep in my room while listening to headphones one night. I was listening to a cassette shortly before I drifted off to sleep. Out of the silence I was awakened my what sounded like an emergency news report coming through the headphones. The problem is that my stereo had been set to cassette making it impossible for the radio stations to suddenly activate without flipping a switch and tuning to an actual radio station.

The voice coming out of my headphones sounded like a reporter claiming that he was trapped in a cave and dying. He would speak about his hatred for life now that he was trapped inside the bowels of the earth. He would utter strange sentences like, "the near-death experiences have started now" and "have a little death, dirt" while explaining his disgust about how the earth always creates violent storms and earthquakes that often kill many people. These statements became increasingly more sinister and frightening. I was fully alert once it began. My eyes were open, and I became so panic-stricken that I could not move. I was convinced that I was losing my mind. It was the middle of the night and everyone was sleeping. My thoughts began to race and became so alien to who I was that I felt they were no longer my own. Something had managed to invade my mind space. Whatever it was didn't care that it was evoking a paralysing terror in me. For all intents and purposes it was my fear that allowed it to grow much stronger and to become more real.

Soon the reporter on the radio would say, "We are getting closer now. We are coming through the walls." As it said that its voice echoed and reverberated out of the headphones and into the room, at least that's what it sounded like to me. As abruptly as the voices began, they stopped. The room suddenly became silent in an instant as though nothing had ever happened. I was horrified beyond measure. I could not be convinced that what I had experienced was just a dream. It was far too real. The quiet stillness that followed was nearly as bad as listening to the voices coming out of the radio. I laid there in expectation of even worse events to come.

The phenomena found a new entry point through my fear. At the time I was too young to understand what was happening. I certainly didn't know where to look for answers. One was limited to the local library for resources to research these types of things. It was a slow process. There was no way to get in contact or even find the experts who dealt with anomalous experiences. What I experienced that night was so outside the normal wavelength of human experience that I wouldn't have been happy with any explanation I was given including the main one I would have heard from my family: demonic influence. I decided my best option was to remain quiet and hope that it wouldn't begin to happen regularly.

I remember at that time thinking that whatever was happening could potentially escalate. I became even more preoccupied by the idea of UFOs and Men In Black at this time because it was the only thing that seemed to define what I had experienced. With a healthy dose of the television show *Unsolved Mysteries,* my mind began to explore more possibilities.

The voice coming through the radio that night was not exactly human. It was too perfect almost like it belonged to a robotic entity that had mastered the English language. It had no accent or impediment of any kind. It was loud, potent, and spoke matter-of-factly. It sounded more like the caricature of a news reporter than an actual news reporter. That is what scared me the most. The mental image my mind conjured during this event was a man that looked like Bob Dobbs, the mascot and prophet of Church Of The SubGenius. The non-humanness of the encounter and the associated emotive power that was released inside of my head, made memories of this event linger in my thoughts for a long time.

After the radio experience things remained quiet again for a time. There was no escalation of strange experiences, just life as usual. All of this would change in June of 1994 on the weekend of my High School graduation when I would have my first most direct experience in normal, waking consciousness of the Harlequin as a young man. It began just a few minutes after I left a graduation party with some friends.

I don't remember what time it was exactly, but it was late and there were very few cars on the road. We were headed north on 76th street and were stopped at the traffic light on 76th and

Oklahoma Avenue on the south-west side of Milwaukee. When the light turned green, we noticed what appeared to be a young woman with blonde hair walking on the east side of the street. She had come out from behind a video store on the corner.

As she walked, we noticed that her movements were very jerky. In those days there was a small park on the northwest corner of that intersection where a few unsavory types used to loiter day and night. It wasn't unusual to see homeless people or drug users in that general area during the summer months. My initial thought was she was possibly a part of that group of people. One of the individuals in my car that evening thought he knew who she was. Even at that moment, the idea that she had a normal name and identity seemed ridiculous to me. Something didn't feel right. As we got closer to her, we began to slow down to get a better look. She took immediate notice of us. Her movements became more exaggerated and violent like a character in a zombie film. With every step she took, her hair bounced more violently tipping us off that she was wearing a cheap wig that at any moment could have fallen off her head revealing something truly horrifying.

We soon realized that nobody in the car knew who this person was. Once again my blood went cold with fear. The feeling of unnerving eeriness fell over us and every moment felt like slow motion dread as we came closer to seeing her face. Everyone was in this quiet state of disbelief because the moment did not jibe with normal human experience. What we witnessed didn't look or act like a person. It acted like someone pretending to be a normal person.

As we crossed paths, she began to walk directly toward my car as if she had a mission. From only a few feet away, I saw her clearly through the passenger side window. There was no mistaking the round mouth and intensity in the large eyes. The Harlequin was wearing a wig and pretending to be a "normal" person walking down the street. From the back seat someone said, "Oh my God her eyes!" A panic struck everyone. I was told to floor it, which I did without hesitation. We flew down 76th Street until we were far enough away to feel somewhat safe. We didn't want her to somehow catch up with us again. That seemed to be an irrational thought since she was on foot and we were in a car. Immediately after we passed her, someone said that she had yelled something at us. I thought I heard her yelling as well. It seemed more like she was telling us something rather than merely barking angrily at us. I would venture to say that we had been warned to back away from her. I don't believe we audibly heard anything despite the appearance that it was shouting violently at us. I believe that everyone had received an intuitive gestalt to promptly leave the area or else. There was a threat of violence in the communicaiton.

Even though we had put miles between us and her, each person struggled to get out of the car that night out of fear that this strange woman might somehow have caught back up to us. Again, that is not a rational fear. It stems from being in the presence of something that transcends mundane experience. It was more primal. Even though most of us were now legally adults, we were still not mature enough to grasp and process the shock that had just went through. There was no frame of reference. Someone said they believed that she was a dead person. I found that to be an apt description of what we saw, at least at that moment because I had no frame of reference. She personified death and the fear of death. It made sense to say it so we could forge some kind of reference point. Her face certainly did not convey the same life force as a living human being. It shook all of us deeply.

After that experience life would end up taking a more ominous tone for everyone that was in the car. One of my friends from that night died of cancer only a few years later. It was diagnosed months after our encounter with the Harlequin. The others ended travelling down dark paths, either becoming addicts or spending time in prison. That night seemed to be an omen for the immediate future.

I am still plagued by the thought of what could have happened if I was on foot that night or if I had stopped the car completely and allowed her to come closer. What if I had run into her alone on that empty street? Would my body have succumbed to the paralysis that overtakes people that witness these types of things? Would I have been taken? To me she was not merely a phantom or a ghost, but something more real. She was the crystallization of everything I feared. I wasn't the only one. Others had now experienced her as well. They felt her overwhelming intensity and the fear she evoked in them. To this day, I cannot say for certain if the Harlequin is male or female. Looking back to the fear I experienced in those days, she could have been compared to the "old hag" or sucubus written about for ages that plagued people in the dead of night with paralytic fear. She could just as easily be any number of catalogued entities that inhabit the unseen realm and periodically invade reality. Cinematically she is the woman in Room 237.

During the summer of 1995 I became a father at the age of 19. I struggled to grow up, to be a dutiful father while still having the maturity of a teenage boy. I worked a menial job while my daughter's mother went to college. Questions began to well up in me. I started to research new ideas and communicate with people that I found strange and interesting. I desperately wanted to understand the reason I was here and what I needed to do. Some of these people helped to give me a better understanding of life, while others were just looking for followers to boss around. I don't know why I suddenly dropped out of the consensus streams of reality. I just know that the inward urge to search for the truth, no matter where it took me, consumed me entirely.

Knowing the proclivities of my childhood friends, I determined it was best to part ways with them forever and stay focused on my family and our well-being. Around 1996 I began to write voraciously. I became interested in old and rare books with topics covering occultism and metaphysics. I found little relief in books that attempted to place the paranormal in neat little boxes. I went deeper into the unknown. I experienced periods of profound insight and unimaginable frustration when the answers evaded me.

One day in 1998 while driving home from work, I had this odd feeling that I was trapped. I was trapped in my car, trapped in my identity, and trapped in the reality I was living in. It was a repeat of my childhood experiences where I saw my neighborhood as a fictitious place, a movie set that wanted me to believe it was real. While in my car, I was suddenly overtaken by the obsessive thought that I was actually in Hell and that my life was a self-generated reality that I designed to protect me from my damnation. In the passenger seat I could feel the presence of someone beginning to manifest. I began to yell at the top of my lungs, "Stop! No! Get the fuck out of my car!" As I raced down the street, I would lift my right foot off the gas pedal and stomp the dashboard breaking off knobs and cracking the plastic. I had fallen into an uncontrollable frenzy of some kind. The terror of death was coming upon me. Every story I read of dark near-death experiences sounded like Disneyland in comparison what I was feeling.

Feeling that I was about to realize I was in Hell without any hope of returning to my blissful mirage of a normal life, I decided to call my girlfriend. When she answered the phone all I could manage to say was, "Help me! I'm all fucked up. Something is happening to me." My girlfriend and mother of my child began to scream in the phone asking what had happened and where I was. I was beside myself. I had no answer to give her because I didn't know myself. Everyone was in Hell along with me. I felt that calling her would somehow fix everything.

Realizing that if I continued to drive this way that I would likely kill someone, I pulled over got out of the car and laid on the grass and begged God to help me. At that point I was covered in a cold sweat. It had been extremely hot all day and out of nowhere this cool breeze came through like a healing wind. I began to calm down. At that point in life my mind was penetrating places that it did not fully understand. This caused intense reverberations that knocked me out of reality altogether and sometimes into panicked states. These types of breakdowns tend to happen to people who are on intense spiritual journeys and are cutting through karmic bonds that are carried down through the generations. As a young child I was initiated into the eternal damnation of hell by my parents. When I was young I believed in that teaching with total confidence. As I got older, my intellectual pursuits qualified me to burn in the lake of fire under my old understanding of things. I had to overcome those beliefs because they had caused me great inner turmoil. For me coming to terms with an understanding of the world and life that was not Christian was a huge hurdle that took years to accomplish.

I was suffering from a spiritual crisis that began in my childhood. I was being forced to answer questions my ancestors refused to answer. I had to process the emotive forces that they refused to deal with. This is the truth in all families. I believed that once I had the proper knowledge of things, I could fix everything and begin to heal myself from grievous wounds against the spirit that would not let me rest.

Now that I was a young father, I was growing increasingly fearful for my baby daughter. I did not want her to be affected by the things that had plagued me and my previous generations. I had family members who suffered from intense spiritual crisis that lead to unstable personal lives and destroyed families. There were early deaths, substance abuse, and a host of unresolved issues. I understood that all of those things existed in me in some way. These things can and will create heavy debts of karma that must eventually be paid in order for there to be peace and wholeness in people who belong to troubled families.

I wanted a lasting resolution. I was not after a half-hearted fix. My ancestors left serious debts that had to be paid. I did not like having that inherited heaviness in my heart all those years. It was agonizing and oppressive and opened doorways into the unseen that I could not shut. As I stated earlier, bad things exist in there as well. Just because something is "spiritual" does not mean it is not malignant and dangerous. It was out of these doorways that the Harlequin and other entities came out of.

As I set out to work through these issues, I began to make friends and contacts everywhere. I used the internet early on when few people saw its value. I became friends with murderers who I wrote to in federal prison. I got to know occultists, pagans, cult leaders, witches, yogis, magicians, hare krishnas, cabbalists, and a slew of others. In some way each of them had pieces of truth (as confused as they all were) and were working out a way to free themselves from their own bondage.   In the late 1990s my associations must have got someone's attention because I was questioned at my home by two men that presented themselves as FBI agents. They wanted to know what I was up to, and if I had any knowledge about plots against the US government.   This became upsetting to members of my family who did not appreciate that kind of attention. Things were growing stranger by the day.

I had officially separated myself from the status quo by the time I was 24. I found kinship with people that were throwaways and pariahs. I loved the people that the world rejected. I felt that it was the minutia of truth these outcasts possessed that pissed everyone off so much. Even now, in 2023, to speak the truth or to state the obvious causes deranged people to lose their minds and cry out for the blood of anyone that doesn't agree with them.   There was something about this angered reaction in people that always interested me. These reactions are a self-designed veil of dishonesty that people use to protect themselves from being truthful and honest. Breaking through that veil means practising absolute honesty about oneself and the world you are living in. All the knowledge gained from books and the writings of the past are nothing in comparison to simple, selfless honesty which will always reveal us for what we really are. Metaphysically, I obsessed over the lies modern culture participates in to keep itself protected from the broader existence that people once (but no longer) belong to. Modern culture and society has been hewn out of the cosmos as a branch cut off of a tree. It lays upon the Earth drying up and passing away while foolishly perceiving that it is itself a mighty tree.

All of my hard pushing for answers alienated those around me. The mother of my child was a normal to a fault. She did not want to stand out or be different. She wanted to be accepted by normal people and have a successful career. Being accepted and having acceptable ideas was never in the stars for me. It bothered me a great deal that she placed such little value on her own experiences often explaining them away in the most sceptical and lackluster ways imaginable. When I urged her on to pursue the meaning of her experiences she wanted no part in it. This is all water under the bridge now and I harbor no animosity toward her.

She was with me one evening when we were abruptly awakened from a deep sleep by what sounded like a helicopter landing on top of our house. She shot up out of bed as a bright light came through our bedroom window. To this day I remember seeing the light beaming against her hair in that moment. She screamed my name in a desperate tone as if I trying to wake me up. I was overtaken almost immediately by paralysis and then the complete darkness of dreamless sleep. She would wake up the next morning only to ask me why I thought the helicopter was flying so low and close to the house. Even though I told her that the event felt like an alien abduction, she dismissed it immediately as if it was all a part of my inherent attraction to the paranormal.

She was with me one day when we had spotted a strange little man walking down the road while stuck in traffic. When the man stared at me, we were both filled with fear in the knowing that this strange person was not human. This man had a hobbit-like appearance not unlike the elvish who are the spirits of the dead taking on a semi-human appearance. Through his stare he communicated to us that he was not to be trifled with. Several young men in the car in front of us saw him as well and began to laugh at his appearance thinking that he was maybe a little person or strange-looking child. When it stared at them they peeled out from their spot into the right lane out of fear. It was no longer funny. My girlfriend and I both intuitively understood that this was an intrusion of something into our reality and it took place on a relatively crowded street. When we got home I was quiet. I explained to her that the man had scared me a great deal. Sitting behind the steering wheel I did everything I could in those moments to not show that I was afraid.

As I stated earlier, I don't think it is fair to say that every manifestation of the paranormal is evil. Things aren't always black and white. I had fallen into the trap of believing that many times in the past. In my case, a great deal of the experiences were "sinister-feeling" but did not significantly harm me. Some of those experiences were placed before me so that I might break through them and gain strength along the way.

There are also less sinister occurrences of the strange that have happened to me when my family was still young. Most memorably was the man in the hot-air balloon. One day we had family over for a cook-out. Everyone was carrying on like usual when suddenly a man in a hot air balloon was directly above us staring down from the basket as he slowly drifted overhead. I could not see a face, but the shadow of his head and shoulders hanging over the basket chilled me to the bone. He was so low to the ground that everyone gasped. Again, there was no continuity to this event. Everything happened so abruptly and out of the blue.

The man in the balloon did not slowly approach us from a long distance away, he just appeared as if he had been there the entire time and we just suddenly noticed him. I remember someone finally breaking the silence of that afternoon by saying, "Well, you don't see that every day." After the balloon was out of sight, everybody just continued on as normal not mentioning or commenting on it again. I found that incredibly odd because with every fiber of my being I wanted to discuss it with people. Those post-event reactions have always puzzled me because they are so mundane. The whole idea of going back to normal after seeing something so out of place only seemed to add to my overall confusion. Yet those are the out-of-place reactions that are documented thoroughly in a great deal of the UFO lore.

A hot-air balloon gliding that close to the ground and appearing suddenly just isn't possible. The burners that fill the balloon with hot air are audible even from the ground so a low-flying balloon "suddenly" appearing without anyone hearing it a distance away doesn't seem plausible. Yet we didn't once hear the propagation of flames the entire span of the encounter and the balloon continued at the same altitude until it was out of sight. How? My answer to that is simple. We were witnessing an intrusion from the unseen realm. The conditions for that day were met that allowed something from the subtle domain to become partially physical. This was not a flesh and blood man piloting the craft, it was something else, a shadow that was revealing itself to everyone. One has to wonder how many events people take as mundane are factually paranormal manifestations. I should also add that the balloon itself had no marking or number, which I believe are required for people who pilot them.

Having others around as witnesses around was always validating. It felt better to tell people that it wasn't just me that saw something out of the ordinary but another person, too. Eventually realizing that I was not losing my mind didn't seem to help matters very much. The growing sense of urgency and paranoia that filled our house in the mid-to-late 1990s was intense. We had even bought Russian surplus night vision goggles which we used to look over the five-acre property at night. Everyone that lived at our house felt apprehensive for reasons they couldn't explain. My daughter's mom to this day believes these security measures were in place because there was a credible threat that serial Killer Angel Resendiz was possibly travelling along nearby railroad tracks.

Inevitably, my hours of studying and research into these matters, my connecting with strange and sometimes dangerous people, and my weird "occult" practices became too much for my daughter's mom to take. I had become an embarrassment to her. In the spring of 2000 we split up and I was told to leave. I had lost everything. One afternoon I came home and all of my things had been packed and waiting for me. I was devastated. When I got home to move my things, my young daughter, then 4 years old, looked up at me and asked, "Daddy, how come you're taking all our stuff?" I was at a loss for words. I swallowed hard and explained it to her the best I could.

I ended up renting a small apartment in Milwaukee. I then had all the time I could ever want for study and research. There would be no interruptions and no complaints about how much time I was spending in my books or conversations I was having with unsavory weirdos. Even though this was what I wanted, I spent the first three months in that apartment alone and in deep despair. I hardly ate or spoke to anyone, my life was reduced to going to work and coming home to sulk in my own misery like a zombie

I began to read dry and tedious spiritual and metaphysical classics that had the quality of being mind-numbingly dry but contained some priceless gems. I would practice meditation almost daily. At first I would just fall asleep and wake up with my head down while drooling on myself. As I began to figure out how it was done, I could hold positions for hours at a time and go places that were unimaginably deep and meaningful. I began to read books like *The Secret Of The Golden Flower* and was eventually able to "hold the light" and concentrate it within myself for extended periods of time. Things inside of me began to change.

When I spoke to people, I understood conversations on a much deeper level. I saw that every conversation began with an imbalance between two people and as it progressed, it moved closer to a state of equilibrium. I could get people to return to a particular topic by speaking in a certain way and ending a conversation at a certain point of imbalance. Beneath every conversation there was always a subtext—the real and hidden point of the conversation. I could pick up on that subtext and bring it up to the surface of my understanding in deep conversations. I was beginning to understand the subtle mechanisms of human relationships and communication. I could tell by interacting with people if they had a good heart or an evil one after only a short period of time. Years of struggle and research were finally starting to pay off.

I began to play with ritual magic at this time. I became very interested in the evocation of spirits into visible manifestation. My apartment during the week looked like a Masonic chamber of reflection. It was a laboratory in which I carried out my research and various practices. I thought I was doing great things. However, I didn't realize I was growing arrogant and elitist in my attitude. Even worse I put my daughter in a great danger without realizing it when she came to visit on the weekends. Luckily, she was never affected by the things I had done.

During this period I would go to sleep at night only to hear knocking from the inside of my closet door. While these manifestations startled me at first, I soon was able to sleep right through them. It was my lack of fear that eventually made them vanish. There were nights when I would see a shadowed man standing in my room or hear what sounded like bells ringing. None of it really shocked me. By that time, I had already seen a lot and was becoming de-sensitized to it. However, there were things that still frightened me.

There was a woman that lived in my apartment complex that frankly scared me to death. She was thin with long black hair. Her face was sullen and she communicated a morose presence. She was probably in her mid 30's at the time. I cannot tell you exactly what about her scared me, but there was something about her that just didn't feel right. I could see something in her "subtext" that bothered me. It seemed that whenever I sat outside, she suddenly popped out to show herself and stare at me with her dead-pan eyes as she walked by. Though she never spoke to me, and I wasn't sure what apartment she actually lived in, it seemed like I was being stalked whenever I came outside. I didn't want to engage in any way because I didn't want to offer her an invitation into my life. My personal fear of her didn't make any sense to me. I still wonder, and perhaps it is a huge stretch, if she was some kind of extension of the Harlequin.

One evening around this time I had an intensely vivid dream that I was driving my car through a nearby town. The roads appeared abandoned and the stores closed. As I forced myself to wake up, I found that I had not been dreaming at all. I was sitting behind the wheel of my car driving after midnight in the town I thought I had been dreaming about. I was confused and disoriented beyond reason. For days I worried if something I had evoked compromised me and made me drive twenty miles away from home in an altered twilight state. The only thing I can add is that I was sleep-deprived for months on end which could have lead to this waking dream.

Around the time of the sleep driving incident, out of place memories were beginning to come to me. Some of these memories were from my childhood and some were of events that I did not remember happening. I began to wonder if whatever was following me was implanting memories into my mind.

In one memory I was in what appeared to be a spaceship hovering high above the earth. I was sitting in a strange room with television screens everywhere. On the screens were brutal images of people being tortured and killed. A woman approached me. Seeing that I was disgusted by the images I saw she said, "there is nothing wrong with looking at moving images of rape and death, Daniel." I was sickened by the memory. The environment of that memory felt like I was in a deep level of Hades where souls were being oppressed by dark entities. I have no idea why the event seemed to come off like I was sitting inside a UFO. It felt like I was sealed up inside of a deep cavern. This typology of a cave was often recurring.

There is another memory of the same dark sort. I am inside of what I am told is a mountain. There are three other men trapped inside and we are all wearing saffron- colored attire. The cavernous room we are in is lit by a couple candles that seem to burn without ever needing new wicks. I understand that I had been trapped in this mountain for entire ages. All of us are slowly dying and have given up all hope of ever getting out. Though we are trapped and dying, I am not frightened or disturbed by what is happening. Even though this sounds like it never happened, it lives on in my mind like an actual memory. It should be mentioned that during the event in 1993 where

I was hearing a reporter on the radio, that he claimed to have also been trapped in a cave. I still don't know the significance of this.

In another memory from my childhood my brother was playing football in a field when he is tackled and falls on a pipe sticking partly out of the ground. The fall did happen and lead to a massive scar on his knee that is still visible to this day. That much is true. I even remember him running home and my dad ripping open his jean leg at the knee and saying, "Oh shit! I can see your bone, kid." But another memory of that day has been slipped in. An aunt drives me and my other brother home from the hospital after my brother is stitched up. We are sitting in the back seat and she orders us to go to the spot where our oldest brother fell so that we can "pick up the skin he lost on the metal pipe and bring it home". We are freaked out by the thought of it but she insists. I don't remember going back to the spot which leads me to believe it is not real. These memories are dark and I have many of them.

More memories began to surface from the first house I was raised in. My brother and I were playing on the front porch and a car pulled up to the curb. My mom was sitting in the passenger seat. An unknown man is driving. We are very puzzled by this because only seconds earlier we saw her in the kitchen. There is no way she could have got in front of us. Whoever this woman was, despite looking identical to my mother, it was not her. She began calling out to me. She wanted me to get in the car and go with her. When she talked, she sounded like my mom but with a recorded, robotic version of her voice. She kept saying that she loved me repeatedly. Seeing that I was suspicious of her, she got back in the car and drove away. As the car drove off I can see her waving goodbye. There was a strong smell that was overwhelming, it smelled like rotten eggs and ozone. It had the putrid electric smell of a blown diode on a circuit board. My brother also remembers this event, but his recollection differs only slightly.

The memory of seeing my mother's doppelgänger has stuck with me for many years now. Whenever I hear stories of young children that go missing, it always floats to the surface. I wonder if the missing leave their homes thinking they are running a simple errand or taking a ride with a parent or friend only to enter into a waking nightmare. I feel that if I had gotten into the car that day or if I had not awoken from the waking dream that took me twenty miles away from home, that I may have never returned. The memory of seeing my mom's doppelgänger and the implication that it was a failed kidnapping event, has lead to an ongoing obsession with missing person stories.

When going over missing person and strange drowning cases like that of Zachary Marr,

Kayelyn Louder, Patricia Meehan and many others, I wonder if these disappearances have a deeper paranormal dimension to them. Were their minds somehow hijacked before they went missing? Was I selected to be the subject of a similar story that would remain unsolved?

Chapter Four:
The Missing

Steph Young

The reader may recall Dan saying: 'When going over missing person and strange drowning cases like that of Zachary Marr, Kayelyn Louder, Patricia Meehan and many others, I wonder if these disappearances have a deeper paranormal dimension to them. Were their minds somehow hijacked before they went missing? Was I selected to be the subject of a similar story that would remain unsolved? ' Are any of the following cases also instances where they found themselves selected?

28-year-old Michael Boyette disappeared in October 2007, in Mobil County. He had been acting out of character prior to his disappearance. It was possible that he was experiencing mental health issues and his family said he did have drug problems. He ran into the woods near his house on Rainbow Lake Road in Grand Bay, and he never returned.

A father of two young children, Lt Paul Burch of the Mobil Sheriff's office said of him: "Earlier in the day, before he ran off into the woods, he'd told his family he was going to "go back where it all started." Despite many official and voluntary searches of woods and the neighbourhood, they could not find him anywhere, and he has never been found.

About a week before he disappeared, Sheriff's deputies were involved in a pursuit with Boyette, when they responded to an attempted suicide complaint. His family said he had thoughts of suicide in the past, but if he had committed suicide, his body would have surely been found? If he is still alive, he has never contacted his family. What did he mean, that he wanted to "go back to where it all started?" Why did he run into the woods?

In April 2004, Jeremy Alex was last was seen running into the woods off Pound Hill Road in Northport, Waldo County, Maine. Prior to this, he had emerged from the woods into the back yard of James and Cynthia Munkelt. Mrs. Munkelt told police the young man was "clutching a wad of money" in one hand and told her, "Bad guys are after me. Don't call the cops."

She phoned the police regardless, out of concern for his welfare. He was distraught, she said, and appeared to be hallucinating. She also recognised him as a former student at the school where she used to work.

Her husband approached him when he appeared in their backyard. Alex told him that bad men were chasing him and were out to get him – but Mr. Munkett could see no sign of these men. He said Alex offered him the bundle of cash to let him go – Munkett was holding on to him, trying to keep him there for his own safety and well-being. But much as he tried to calm the young man down, Alex broke free from his grip and ran back into the woods. Munkett said he appeared to be paranoid and terrified.

That was the last time anyone saw him. Waldo County Detective Jason Trundy said that Alex appeared to recognize the Munketts one minute and not know who they were the next. He added that nothing credible to explain his disappearance had been given to them in terms of information. Despite a $20,000 reward offered by his family, no-one came forward to claim it. The detective said the young man had mentioned an argument with his girlfriend. Alex's girlfriend, Suzanne Forqueran said that her last conversation with him earlier that day "wasn't a good conversation. He was not in his right mind."

He'd been in the process of moving his possessions into their new home in Harbor Road that day. Detective Trundy said Alex had been known to use a variety of drugs. The search for him had included 6 K-9 teams from Maine Search and Rescue, members of the Sheriff's Department and Maine Game Wardens. A plane was also used. The search lasted for a full four days. His family and friends failed to find any sign of him either. A further search in the woods twenty weeks later, revealed nothing.

His family called him 'a free spirit' but he was close to them and his girlfriend. They said he was not known as a person who would get paranoid or frightened before. But, he'd run off from their new house, leaving his truck behind, his cell phone behind and his keys hanging in the front door.

Lagniappe, Mobile Alabama's independent weekly newspaper reported on the disappearance of another young man named Jeffrey Holloman. "When Jeffery Holloman left his home on August 2nd 2011, he was under the influence of "something." His wife reported that he was hallucinating that there were people in the trees in their front yard. Armed with a baseball bat, he ran off to get the "people."

His wife subsequently filed a missing person's report with the police, when he didn't come back. Days later he was picked up by officers in George County, Mississippi. Unfortunately, at the time, the officers who stopped him hadn't received the missing person's alert. They drove him to the Alabama state line where he then set off on foot again. This was the last time he was seen. Deputies reportedly walked the roads that Holloman should have taken and searched the woods around the area, but found no sign of him. He's still missing.

17-year-old Kurt Sova went missing from a party on October 23rd 1981, in Newburgh Heights, Ohio. Kurt had been drinking at the party and stepped outside with his friend Samuel to get some air. After he vomited, his friend went back inside the party to collect their jackets and take him home. When Samuel returned, Kurt was gone.

His friend looked all around, walked the nearby streets, but on finding no sign of him he presumed that Kurt had already started walking home while he was inside the house. The next morning Kurt's parents discovered he had not come home. They searched for him, checking the streets, back yards, dumpsters and local wooded area. Two days after the party, the police began their search for him.

Two days later, a homeless man walked into a record shop in the small town. He'd been hanging around outside for a couple of weeks. The homeless man said that he had "access to bodies flown in" to the nearby Cleveland Hopkins International Airport. He bragged about stealing the shoes from 'the bodies.'

He walked up to the store manager Judy Oros, and pointed to Kurt's missing person's poster, which was on display in the store window. He told her; "They're going to find him and they're going to find him in two days and they're not going to know what happened to him."

Two days later, three school kids cut through the woods behind the furniture store opposite the Party House, on their way home from school. They spotted what looked like a discarded shop Mannequin, lying half-in and half-out of the river. It was lying in a crucifixion pose.

On closer inspection, it wasn't a mannequin at all; it was Kurt's body. Cleveland newspaper The Plain Dealer later reported that his body was "Cruciform; arms outstretched, head to one side, one knee slightly bent and one foot atop the other."

Patrolman Paul T. Grzesik said, "When we arrived there, his body was laid out like Christ on the cross. One shoe was found nearby. We never found the other (right) shoe."

Eventually, the right shoe would be found positioned inside a pile of rocks nearby, in what would seem a deliberate manner. The coroner later determined that the boy had a bruise on his cheek, bruises on his shins and minor abrasions. However, he had no fatal injuries - no knife wounds, or bullet wounds, or needle marks, and no internal injuries. The coroner was unable to find a cause of death.

The next day, the homeless man returned to the record store, carrying a bunch of flowers. With the flowers was a card. It said: "Roses are red, the sky is blue, they found him dead and they'll find you." Who was this homeless man, and what did he really want?

Three months later, schoolboy Eugene Kvet's body was found in a ravine 2.5 miles from the ravine in which Kurt's body had been found. His right shoe was also missing. He had been missing for roughly the same amount of time as

Kurt. His cause of death was presumed to be from falling into the ravine, but like Kurt, he had only minor abrasions.

30-year-old Teleka Patrick had gained a medical degree, a Ph.D. in biochemistry, and had research published. Professor D. DeLeon, her mentor at Loma Linda University called her "brilliant." Following completion of her research at the university in California, she began a four-year residency in psychiatry at University School of Medicine in Kalamazoo.

But there was another very troubling side to Teleka, that no-one knew about, apart from those most closely and unwillingly involved. It came to be more widely known after she disappeared. In early December 2013, she vanished. On the night of December 5th, 2013, for some reason she attempted to check in at the downtown Radisson Plaza Hotel, Kalamazoo, even though she had her own accommodation not far away. Security footage captured her standing at the reception desk for fifteen minutes. Teleka failed to book the room because she did not have her credit card on her at the time and did not have sufficient cash.

She got the shuttle bus service back to her medical residency where her car was parked. Her car was found two hours later abandoned in a ditch 100 miles away, on the 1-94 in Portage, Indiana. A motorist reported seeing her car off I-94, telling investigators the vehicle was being driven erratically before it went off the road. The car keys were gone.

She was reported missing the following day when she failed to arrive for work. Her cell phone was found at work. Later it would be revealed that police found clothing, as well as her ID, credit cards and wallet, inside the car. The previous day, a co-worker said she'd received a phone call, after which her demeanour changed. Her family offered a

$10,00 reward for information about her whereabouts.

In April 2014, four months later, her body was discovered in Lake Charles in Porter, east of Gary, Indiana. Police and the FBI had previously searched the lake on January 23rd but had found nothing related to her disappearance. No signs of trauma or foul play were found on the body. Her cause of death appeared to be drowning. Two autopsies later confirmed asphyxiation by drowning.

Her ex-husband, Smiley Calderon, who lived in Orange, California said in interviews that he had tried to get her to seek psychiatric help in 2009, but that her response had been to file for divorce from him. He said she was worried that a diagnosis of mental illness would ruin her medical career.

For her parents and friends, there were many unanswered questions about what happened to Teleka. She lived just three miles from the hotel she'd tried to book into, so they could not understand why she had been trying to stay there. She'd tried to check in by paying with money she'd borrowed from a friend rather than use her own credit card. They couldn't understand why she would leave her cell phone at work and her ID and credit card in her car, then go to the hotel. They didn't know why her car had come off the road.

A few weeks after she went missing, videos surfaced on YouTube of Teleka making 'breakfast for two' and talking to the camera as though talking to a lover, but it was believed she was alone at the time.

It was also revealed that she had an unhealthy obsession for a Preacher. Grammy-nominated widower, Reverend Marvin Sapp appeared to have become the object of her affection, to such an alarming degree that he'd sought to take out a protection order on her after she'd turned up at his home where his children also lived. She had apparently been stalking him by one means or another, for over a year, after joining his church when she moved to Kalamazoo. She claimed that Sapp was her husband, which of course, he was not.

Teleka was very active on social media, as it turns out, under a number of pseudonyms. She was sometimes open in expressing that she believed she might be having a psychotic break. She thought that messages posted by Rev. Sapp on his social media platforms and intended for his wide audience in general, contained coded messages specially to her. She also believed her was sending her telepathic messages.

She tweeted: "God connected us again. And I was able to hear your thoughts in my head and communicate with you by thought. We could both do it. And you were able to be inside of my mind." She also believed God was directly communicating with her: "God said jump I said how high?"

But what is perhaps of most concern is her messages about demons. "You reach me through a demonic portal. That gives demons power over me and dilutes my spiritual authority ... Please understand that I must protect myself spiritually. Because you are using a demon to contact me, when I turn my heart towards you, it passes through a demonic power. My authority in the spirit realm and my ability to cover will be markedly decreased. When I say I love you, I am also saying I love you to a demon."

Talking to God presumably, she writes: 'I would honestly like to be controlled by your spirit at all times. Thank you for showing me that there are ugly parts of me that need to be changed. Not fixed, but Killed. Because you can't do anything with my flesh. There's no protection so I have to be a lot more careful."

On the 4th of December, she submitted an article on spirituality and psychiatry for the

American Psychiatric Association Annual Meeting. On the 5th of December, the day of the evening that she disappeared, she deactivated all of her twitter accounts. Was it mental illness, a psychotic break, stress from over-work? Was it unrequited love, spiritual fervour, or something far more malign, that led her-to-death?

Twenty-six-year-old Emma Fillipoff disappeared off the streets of Victoria, British Columbia, on November 28th, 2012. She left journals behind, and all her worldly possessions. In her journal she wrote: "I feel like there's someone following me. A car that was on the hill drove off after it paused in the street. I feel like I'm being stalked." She did have a stalker a few months earlier, who had even written to her parents to apologise for his behaviour.

She'd moved to the city a few months prior to disappearing. She was jobless and struggling financially after working only briefly at a seafood restaurant. She was living in a women's shelter in the City. She was last seen talking to police outside a hotel in the centre of town. Prior to this, earlier in the day she'd gone to her local convenience store. She was captured on the security cameras entering the store and as she paid for a new cell phone at the counter. She was then seen hovering by the door, peering outwards as if she is looking for someone outside. She leaves the store but immediately returns. She repeats this action several times.

She then caught a cab some time later, asking to be taken to the airport but quickly she realised she didn't have enough money to pay for the ride. The driver offered to take her somewhere else but she couldn't make her mind up where to go.

Later, at around 7.30 pm she was seen by two acquaintances walking in the street. They thought she appeared distressed and confused and they enquired if she was ok. They noticed she was barefoot. Failing to be reassured by her answers, they called the police. After spending about half an hour talking to her, the police decided that although she did appear confused and distressed, they did not feel she was a danger to herself or others and they left. That was the last time she was seen.

Her van was left in a parking lot in the City, with all of her belongings including her passport, camera, art work, laptop and clothes. Her journals were also there. The police questioned her stalker, and a person who later used her credit card, but both passed polygraphs.

Her last journal entry reads: "Hell is all around me... I chased death all my life because I was dead." Why does she say this?

Chapter Five:

Sinister Awakenings

Dan Mitchell

By the summer of 2000 I would begin dating the woman I would eventually marry and have three children with. I ended up landing a decent and stable job that allowed us to live comfortably. My life was finally beginning to stabilize. I was networking online and in person with others like me. During this time, I met an individual that I will call John. Of all the people that I had known with interests in occultism, alternative history, magic and the like, he seemed to be a cut above the rest. Aside from being well-read and in control of himself, he worked for a military contractor and made a good living. He was a widower having lost his wife to a congenital heart defect.

John was 17 years older than me and had a collection of amazing stories. He would tell them in such a way that you would have no choice but to believe what he was telling you. He had hundreds of pictures of himself in interesting places and with interesting people. He spoke with authority and there was this unmistakable power in him. He became a kind of den father to me and several of my friends and associates. He told us that he belonged to a club that was not open to the public. You could only become a member by invitation only. This club sounded more like a secret society one might see in a movie. He explained that there were no meetings or dues of any kind. Once in you were in it, you were in it for life. John appeared to be a recruiter of some kind. When we pressed him for more information, he would tell us that he was sworn to secrecy. It was the only story of his that I ever doubted. He was always building up a mystique about it.

I sometimes wondered if John was able to hide his trauma better than most of us. I was never one to blindly believe in stories that people told me or to accept ideas I could not prove for myself. So there was always a persistent doubt that I had in people like John no matter how believable they were.

Some of the stories John told us were genuinely terrifying. They painted a picture of the world that I hadn't previously been exposed to. More importantly his stories seemed to explain a great deal of my strange childhood memories. For John the world was not what it appeared to be. He once told me that the demon core event that took place on May 21st, 1946 at a Los Alamos Laboratory was a ritual event. He claimed that Louis Slotin was a cabalist magician with a swollen ego. He explained that the study of exotic nuclear materials was not simply about creating nuclear weapons, but of ritualistic and alchemical experiments that employed these materials to initiate contact with dangerous entities. For John the real type of magic, the stuff that worked, required exotic materials. Whether it was historic relics of dead civilizations or a 6-kilogram spherical mass of Plutonium, these items had ritual significance even in our present time. The world he presented to me was strange and novel. This was many years before "fakeology" and conspiracy came into the mainstream.

One day he invited me to attend a gathering. He said it was initiatory in nature and that my attending would be beneficial. The only requirement was that I was to wear no printed clothing. I was to dress as neutral as possible. In my mind this was going to be a convocation of larpers and renaissance fair geeks dancing around or singing. I had been to enough events of this nature with John to know that this was the norm. Whether it was sacred music gatherings, ceremonial gatherings, religious gatherings, or speaking engagements by obscure authors, I was convinced that there was nothing new under the sun. By that time, I had been to so many of these venues that I had grown tired of them.

After a long drive, we pulled into the driveway of this amazing old stave church. On each side of the driveway there were these enormous wood stakes in the ground. One was carved as a bear, and the other as a crow. The structure was on private property and had a gravel parking lot. It was not very big, but it had a rustic feel to it. I remember commenting to John how amazing this place was and asking him if it was a church. He looked to me and said, "It's a church...of sorts."

Getting out of the vehicle I could hear a large bass drum thumping from inside. I remember approaching the building and feeling a sense of foreboding. I looked over to John and asked him what was going on? "Just wait." He responded. "Everything is fine." My anxiety must have been transparent. That he wasn't saying much was making me extremely agitated. There were a few cars parked outside, not nearly as many as I would have expected for a gathering of typical social outcasts. Whatever was happening this time felt very different. This was not a gathering of musicians, chaos magicians from the Illuminates of Thanteros, or occult authors. This felt different.

As we walked through the door I saw five men standing in the back of the church on the small stage. I remember feeling the muscles in my abdomen tighten up. There was this amazing smell in the air, very similar to sandalwood. Four of the men in the back were wearing dark robes and appeared to have black cloth bags over their heads with a rope that cinched the bags around their necks. The fifth man standing in the middle and slightly in front of the four was covered from head to toe in a black robe. He wore a tall, pointed hood that had two eye holes cut out. The lighting in the church was very dim so it was difficult to figure out what was happening those initial moments. I could see the white bass drumhead in the corner, but now everything was mostly silent as we stood at the doorway. Those initial moments felt eerie because everyone was staring at us in complete and utter silence. I felt petrified.

Directly in front of us (between the front door and the five men standing in the back) there were people in multi-colored gowns. The gowns were somewhat shiny as they reflected some of the dim light in the room. These were men and women, in equal number, not wearing anything over their heads. The men had short hair and beards, and the women had exceptionally long hair. They all appeared older than I was, possibly early to mid 40s, the age I am now. None of them were overweight or out of shape. They had a solid appearance. I believe there were 14 people in total kneeling, but there may have only been 12. My memory of them betrays me. I believe these people in the front were meant to symbolize syzygys. Females were on one side and males were on the other. Each man faced a woman.

John quietly began to speak to me, and as he did I heard the people begin to shuffle around a bit. I was told that I should walk slowly through the middle between where the men and women were facing each other. Before I did that I had to only remove my jacket. John made it clear that I should not remove my shoes as that is a gesture of surrender. He told me to walk up to the man with the pointy hood. Once I was about 3 feet in front of him, I was to drop to my right knee and bow my head. He warned me not to look this man in the eye once I knelt. From there I was to follow the man's instructions and answer his questions. There were no complex gestures or sayings I had to memorize. The event was very direct and simple. Extemporaneous.

As I began to walk forward, the men and women began to chant toward one another. As I walked directly through their chanting, I immediately began to understand that this symbolized my being born into existence and polarities being put into my soul. I didn't simply understand it, I felt it. The chanting had a haunting sound to it. There were no words, it was more like smooth and rhythmic tones being vocalized and vibrated into the air. My hearing them was to cause changes in my subtle body, my soul.

As I got closer to the man in the pointed hood, I had this terrible feeling in the pit of my stomach. This was unlike the things I had previously seen and been a part of. The people in that room seemed deadly serious to me. I could feel it. They were not larping by any stretch of the imagination. Whomever they were, they exuded this unmistakable presence and nobility of spirit that shook me quite badly.

When I finally reached the back of the church, I had a better view of the men standing there. Their robes were very nicely embroidered with various symbols, many of which surround the figure of the bear. The bear was extremely significant to them. Upon closer examination the four men standing slightly to the rear of the man in the pointed hood were wearing nooses around their necks. These nooses cinched the cloth bags they were wearing over their heads. I did not take this to symbolize a threat to me, but it was a part of their ethos and mythology.

Upon my approach to the man in the middle, I got a good long stare at his veiled face. His stare, the closer I got, frightened me. I did not need to be coached to drop to my right knee. I was going to drop to my right knee naturally.

My bending the knee was in no way contrived, it was done out of a mix of fear and humility in the presence of a man whose eyes communicated an other-worldly strength. I would post articles on Luminosity about this man and variously describe him as a devil, or a psychopath, or even the Harlequin itself. However, that was not so. This person was a man, a human being, and by his questions and presence, he lived by a particular code that he desired to pass on to me.

I felt as if he was veiled because he could not be looked upon without evoking fear in a human being. I remembered the story of Moses after he had been in the presence of Yahweh. His kinsmen could not look upon him because his countenance had instilled terror. Moses wore a veil to protect the people from seeing a face that had beheld God. I have often wondered what happened to this man that gave him such a striking countenance that was communicated through the intensity of his eyes alone.

The man began an oration aimed at everyone in the room. His voice had this thundering quality to it. When he pronounced certain words, they bounced off of the walls and deflected back at me. This made me jump very slightly. I felt like covering my ears but was too fearful to do so.

He began to ask me a series of moral questions. He asked if I had plotted in secret to defame or harm my friends or family. He asked if I was a "liar to myself" or if I had ever harmed a living thing due to an inner "sexual hunger" to inflict pain. His questions seemed to be asking if I was a potential serial killer, a criminal, a pervert, a liar, or an honest man. I found the questions to be uncomfortable at times but not intolerable. Then his oration changed once again.

He then asked me to stand so that we could "speak as men". I felt terrified to my core. It felt like I was a child again looking into the angered face of my father. He asked me one last question before we were finished. He asked,

"Do You Know The Mystery Of God's Sorrow?"

My response was that I did not. I was then given the charge to search for the answer to this "holiest of questions" and to depart. I turned around and began to walk toward the door where I saw John kneeling and looking down at the wood floor. As I walked out there was this dead silence on the part of everyone in the room. I had never seen or experienced anything like it. It was real magic, real power and I had just been initiated into it. These were not people that drew magical circles on the floor and begged spirits to appear before them. They did not buy or study modern books on magic, traditionalism, or occultism. They were something else entirely. John stood up from a kneeling position as I approached, and we left.

After walking out of the stave church there was once again the thumping of the bass drum. I was told to not look back. The entire event couldn't have been any longer than twenty minutes.

Once in the car I remembered asking him what I had just been put through. I was grilling him harshly about the man in the pointy hood. I got extremely upset that I had not been allowed to prepare for it. He explained that my being prepared would have defeated the purpose of the initiation. He remained stoic and said very little despite my obvious hostility. He added that I did very well and was now a part of something real. In his words, the people in that church did not advertise for membership online or in ads. This was something different. This was the club he had been building a mystique around for so long. When I asked him what I was now supposed to do, he said I was to do nothing.

"It's already been done. You just need to move forward."

When I got home that night, I was unable to sleep. There was a definite change in me. I began tossing out many of my old books because I knew they were garbage. I discarded many of my implements because I began to view many of the ritual practices I was into as childish and moronic. Whatever had happened to me that day reoriented something inside of me. It felt as if some karmic debt had been paid. I was going to move forward, just like I was told.

Years later the events that took place in the stave church would become infinitely more important to me. Even now, all these years later, many revelations about them have come to me.

I would now like to relate a story that happened only a few months after the stave church incident. A friend of mine named Jason had been missing for a couple weeks. Jason was a musician in a local Milwaukee band. He was troubled in the sense that he could not hold down a job and always took things so personally. If he received any kind of criticism it would deeply wound him. I cannot say whether he had a fragile ego or if there was a deeper cause for this flaw in his personality. I can only say that he was hurting and it was impossible to make him feel better about things. It was not unusual for him to just disappear like that as he was struggling with addiction. He normally had several months of sobriety followed by binges where nobody knew where he was. His cousin called because he needed a ride to pick Jason up from a house on the other side of the state near the Mississippi river.

For the entire ride Jason's cousin said very little. There weren't many details to the story he gave me other than Jason had been partying and had been awake for days. Now crashing hard, he called his cousin for a ride home. By the time we found the house, it was already dusk. It was a relatively normal looking home in an upper middle-class residential area.

As I got out of the car, I noticed that Jason's cousin had remained in the car. I knocked on the window and asked if he was coming. He shook his head and seemed set on waiting in the car. I began walking toward the house. On my approach I heard Jason's cousin yell something to me, "watch out for their faces, they got blood on their faces." I wasn't sure that I had heard him correctly. As soon as I got out of the car, I heard music coming from inside of the house. The closer I got I noticed the song seemed out of place. It was Bobby Sherman's, "Julie Do You Love Me?", hardly the kind of song that Jason's crowd would listen to.

I rang the doorbell several times and a young woman came to the door. I noticed others were lingering in the background as well. I was nervous because the lights seemed dim in the house. The young woman at the door seemed out of her mind. Her eyes were wide-open like she was afraid to blink. Her face was covered in what appeared to be dried blood or possibly feces. I was revolted by it completely. The smell inside the house was terrible. I told her that I was looking for Jason and she let me in. An uneasiness fell over me. As I waited in the foyer, I saw one of the ladies in the background put her hand down the front of her pants and then quickly rub her face and the face of the another lady in front of her. My first impression was that I was surrounded by people on a meth binge, and that is likely what was happening. What Jason's cousin had told me before, about blood being on their faces, suddenly made sense to me. The young women in the house were rubbing menstrual blood on their faces. If Jason had told his cousin this detail on the telephone when he called for help, he didn't make me aware of it until we arrived.

I would have felt otherwise about going into the house that evening.

The song on the stereo kept repeating over and over. After a while, it felt like nobody was getting Jason for me and I was growing increasingly disturbed and agitated. I began to walk further into the house. Numerous times the women would just run right by me like I wasn't there. It was like they were playing tag inside of the house. There were either 4 or 5 of them in the house, possibly more upstairs. At one point, one of them put her arm around me, the same woman that answered the door. I cautiously pushed her away out of fear of getting blood on me. I once again asked her where Jason was and if she could let him know that his ride had arrived. She just made odd statements that had no meaning to them. I realized things were going nowhere. I was going to have to get Jason myself. However, by that point I had no idea if he was even in the house and I really didn't want to start checking rooms out of fear of what I might see. It felt like I had entered the twilight zone.

Initially I hadn't seen or heard any men while I stood inside the foyer, but I could sense more people in the house. As I walked further in, I had this sense that it was not drugs causing these women to be in hysterics. It was as if they were overtaken by fear and could not leave the house. I could feel the delusions they were trapped in. Seeing them made me feel as though I was witnessing a ritualistic event, something dark-natured and oppressive. Their panicked and agitated state gave them the appearance of dark priestesses or oracles speaking the words and dictates of their Lovecraftian old ones. These were intuitive impressions I was receiving during those initial moments.

I walked into the large living room and saw a large stone fireplace. There was a man sitting there on the couch but I did not want to look at him. I remember reaching in my jacket pocket which must have looked obvious. I had grown accustomed to carrying a slapjack at times like this just in case I ran into any trouble. Jason was always trouble so this was a precaution on my part. Once I saw the man I didn't feel right. The man in the living room immediately told me that whatever was in my pocket was of no use to me inside his house. The voice was neither male nor female. It sounded androgyne and neutral-much like a robot might sound.

From that point forward my memories become cloudy. I have never used drugs, but I remember feeling terrified that one of the women had somehow drugged me. In the memories that follow, there are sometimes three men in that room. Other times I only remember one. Even though in this man's presence I felt that I had been drugged, I never felt a needle and I never ate or drank anything from the house. I had been drinking from a bottle of water that had not once left my sight.

The sense I had of the man in the living room was a person that was not human. Even though I refused to look at him, my mind's eye painted a portrait of a person not unlike the Harlequin from 1994. It was just wearing another disguise. I saw a silver-haired man sitting on the couch. He was rail thin, pallid skin, and wearing clothes that were too big for him. He looked out of place there. Sometimes I get the impression that he was a corpse and not a living man.

It felt as though he was feeding off the fear and hysteria happening inside the house. He was a revenant and I could sense that he was extremely dangerous. Deep down I knew these girls were not allowed to leave the house. The thought of them being trapped really freaked me out. The repeating song in the background just added to the overall insanity of what I was seeing and intuitively grasping.

My memory of that day has faded out a great deal. What I remember was the feeling of electricity going through my spine which has been the main physical symptom of nearly all malevolent attacks I have experienced throughout my life. The next thing I knew was that I was walking out of the house with Jason in tow and we were struggling through disorientation to get to the car. I never saw him come out of any rooms nor did I hear his voice the entire time I was in the house. We were just suddenly together and leaving the house. Could this have been a subdued panic reaction on my part? That is possible. I had never been in that type of environment and admit that I was deeply concerned for my safety.

As we drove back home I grilled Jason's cousin about how he knew the girl's faces were going to be covered in blood. He denied that he ever said anything about blood. The most likely explanation was that Jason called his cousin and told him about the weirdness going on in the house. This was why he refused to come inside with me. He already knew it was going to be too weird or scary for him. During the car ride home, I asked Jason question after question. I wanted to know how he had gotten there, who the people in the house were, and what had happened inside. My inquiries were met by silence or "I don't knows." He didn't remember much.

That evening has stuck with me for years and revealed the ambiguous nature of paranormal experiences. For me the one true detail that validates the paranormal part of that day is the discontinuity and disjointedness once I got inside. Knowing that paranormal events can be forgotten or manipulated after the fact, I have kept journals to remind me of the details so things don't get lost.

There are other problems as well. Like many high-strangeness events, there are no conclusions or real answers to be had. Everything is ambiguous. People are left in a state of uncertainty because the conscious mind is not able to process these events very well. It tends to cover them up or re-write them over long periods of time. If I can say anything about what took place that day with Jason, it is that I felt to be under some kind of hypnosis where I was left powerless. Even if I wanted to I couldn't have defended myself against someone or something harming me.

According to a conversation I had with Jason years later, he had been awake for days on meth. He didn't know who all the women were at the house that day, but stated he met an older women in a bar weeks earlier and they "hit it off." They spent several days together and drove across the state to that house together. Their trip was under the pretense that she needed to pick up money from a relative. Once they arrived at the house things became blurry. He couldn't say if he was there for two days or a week. Furthermore, he didn't remember seeing any thin, strange-looking man being in the house at any time, at least nobody that looked like the corpse that I saw. To Jason who was used to living life on those terms, his stay in that house was nothing out of the ordinary.

One detail did stick out, however. He claimed that the women I saw that day arrived the first night he was there. He explained that they personally knew (or were related to) the woman he drove there with. That same night, the woman stepped out and never returned to the house, stranding Jason on the other side of the state. The young women wanted to party despite Jason's predicament. As the party was getting started, the women told him that they were part of a popular dance troupe out of

Illinois. As the evening progressed, one of them began to have a deep conversation with Jason about topics of an other-worldly nature. She told Jason that she gave birth to a reptilian hybrid child when she was younger, and that it was taken from her and placed on a different planet. She told him that her family had distant reptilian lineage and that an abortion doctor in the Midwest, whom she personally knew, procured fetuses that were somehow revived, incubated, and grown into gray aliens. Jason did not believe her for a second and felt creeped out by her because she spoke nonchalantly about dark things.

I was standing in very close proximity to these young women that day and did not have a good feeling about them at all. Even if they were trapped in a drug-induced delusion after being awake for days, there is something about the way they were gliding through the house that made it feel "ritualistic" and purposeful. I have always felt that it was some kind of dark oracle at work. The terrifying desperation that was on their faces didn't help. Did I arrive and stop something that was going to happen? Was I somehow hypnotized by something in the house that has caused me to forget details about the conversation I had with the corpse? Like every other story of this nature, there is no proper ending or conclusion.

Chapter Six:

The Revenant

Steph Young

Recalling Dan's encounter with the man at the house: 'His skin was pale, his countenance was pallid. He seemed to be alive, but wasn't. He was some type of revenant and I could sense that he was very dangerous,' the deadliest use of magic can come in the form of the creation of a Revenant.

Says Dan; 'A revenant is a magically created being. Similar to a golem.' A revenant at its most fundamental is believed to be a ghost that can be visibly seen, or, a re-animated corpse that is believed to have been revived from death to serve a spell caster, or rather, a necromancer.

Necromancy can involve the practice of raising a body from the dead through magic, then using that deceased person to do their bidding, usually for nefarious and sinister means.

Revenants are perhaps at first glance best recognised through the Voodoo tradition. The Haitian's have a strong basis in folklore and perhaps in truth, of the possibility of reanimated but soulless corpses. The zombie, created from the freshly-dug corpse is the slave of its master, the bokor. It breathes, can speak, can hear, but it possesses no memory of its former-self, and no comprehension of the creature it has become. It does not have a consciousness as we do. It is a biological robot.

American occultist, explorer, traveller, and occasional cannibal, William Seabrook once described an experience he had in Haiti in 1918. He was led by a farmer through sugar crop fields where the farmer, Constant Polynice, who had once renounced the idea of 'Zombies' as nonsense, stopped close to a group of three men. The men were digging the ground with machetes, under the supervision of a young woman.

The American occultist looked into the face of one of the men and said: "What I saw then, came as rather a sickening surprise. Their eyes were the worst. It was not my imagination. They were in truth like the eyes of a dead man, not blind, but staring, unseeing. The whole face seemed not only expressionless but incapable of expression."

Some authorities believe that such examples of 'Zombies,' particularly during the Haitian labour shortage of that era, were actually people who had been drugged into a coma, buried and then dug up again and revived with other drugs. Before selling their victims, the sorcerers were said to have then cut out their tongues so that they could not reveal their true origins.

Skinwalkers it is said, are necromancers, who raise the dead and create revenants. Professor of anthropology, Clyde Kluckhohn wrote 'Navaho Witchcraft' in 1944 after spending more than three decades researching and interviewing Navaho people. He collected very rare accounts of Skinwalkers and their practices, using highly rigorous parameters to ensure as much accuracy and veracity as possible. Some of the testimonies he received were both chilling and appalling;

'Witches are associated with death and the dead. References to male witches are more numerous. Killing a close relative is their initiation. A preparation is made from the flesh of corpses, with the flesh of children preferred, and this 'corpse poison' is ground into powder. When administered, fainting, unconsciousness, or worse is usually said to result very quickly.'

'These 'Were-animals' meet at night to initiate new members, to have intercourse with dead women, to practice cannibalism, and to kill victims at a distance by ritualized practice. It is often in a cave, where they sit in a circle surrounded by baskets of corpse flesh. Some witnesses said that rows of recognizable human heads were seen there. Sorcery, essentially 'enchantments' or 'spells' ideally need a victim's offal; hair, nails, faeces. This will be buried with flesh or other material from a grave.'

'The dead bodies are gone and the wolf tracks are around it. Witches aren't afraid of graves - they are their homes. They go there while the meat is still fresh. They tear the grave open and bring out the body. One time this hunter came along that I used to know. He was lost and he went right in to the place where they were meeting to ask for directions. He soon found out he was in a place he had no business to be in. He stayed inside long enough to think what he would do. These people had killed a fine woman. A day after she died they had taken her to this witchery hogan. They put her body behind a blanket in one corner and one after another the witch men had intercourse with her.

The hunter could hear one man after another saying, "Now she's getting warm."

A Hindu sect known as the Aghori's are also believed to indulge in secret rituals of black magic necromancy, with sex in graveyards being a major component. The female partners are smeared with the ashes of the dead. They perform rituals over the newly dead and "marry" that dead person to them, binding its death force to enhance their own supernatural powers.

In the 1100's, Reverend William of Newburgh wrote of Revenants and Vampires in Historia rerum Anglicarum, in which he says: 'It would not be easy to believe that the corpses of the dead should sally (I know not by what agency) from their graves, and should wander about to the terror or destruction of the living, and again return to the tomb, did not frequent examples, occurring in our own times, suffice to establish this fact, to the truth of which there is abundant testimony. Were I to write down all the instances of this kind, the undertaking would be beyond measure...'

In Historia Rerum Anglicarum they often drink blood, like the Vampire lore, and corpses of revenants can be found swollen and suffused with blood. Particularly during the middle ages, texts describe the belief that corpses were coming back to life. They would rise from their graves at night and roam the lands, seeking people to terrorize. Derived from the Latin 'Reveniens' and the French 'Revenir' they meaning of the Revenant is 'those who come back.'

Newburgh includes examples such as at Alnwick Castle in Northumberland, England where during the 1200's the people who lived there began to be terrorized by a corpse who rose at night from its tomb in the graveyard. Reverend Newburgh wrote of the accounts of this creature that plagued them: A man, after his death, and despite being given a Christian burial and laid to rest in the cemetery near the Castle, began to cause reports of travellers crossing the countryside alone on horseback or foot, only to be accosted by the most hideous sight of a corpse coming out of the forest, and hurling itself at them, scratching and slashing at his victims as they fought to defend themselves against the corpse.

As the accounts grew, the terrified locals refused to travel alone in the countryside at night and even when in pairs or groups, they would be terrified of passing any trees or bushes, nervous that the corpse would jump out on them and attack them next. They waited until Palm Sunday came around and when it did, a group of the most devout residents were led on a procession to the Cemetery. Among them also were the bravest men in the area, who armed themselves with sharp sticks and spades, ready to attack the revenant should it rear its head and make its presence felt as they made their way to the cemetery.

Once there, they proceeded to dig up the grave of the revenant, recoiling in shock at the sight of the corpse which appeared fresh as though it had just been buried that very moment. Even worse, there was fresh blood around its lips. The men dragged his body out of the grave and cut off his head, then dragged the decapitated body out of the graveyard and took it a long distance away, where they lit a funeral pyre and burnt his body.

King James VI of Scotland, in his Daemonologie, of 1597, a treatise on Necromancy, believed that a demonic entity could possess a dead person, although he was also heavily involved in the witch trials so perhaps was not impartial. In the 1700's Augustine Calmet wrote that walking corpses were not isolated incidents, according to the people he spoke with across the countries of eastern Europe while researching for his book Traité sur les apparitions des espirits et sur les vampires ou les revenans.

He wrote: "It is said that men who have been dead for several months, come back to walk and infest, (making) ill use of men and beasts. These revenants come out of their tombs. People can only save themselves from these dangerous visits by impaling them and cutting off their heads, and tearing out their hearts.'

Were all of these reports really so, or, was it that those buried had not been dead all along – but accidentally buried prematurely, when contagious diseases ravaged and people could fall into fever and then comas? Despite modern interpretations of Calmet's writing seeking to support the phenomenon of revenants and vampires, in fact at times Calmet expressed his own scepticism, upon failing to find solid proofs despite questioning local people wherever a 'revenant outbreak' might have occurred. On the other hand, the hundreds of witnesses to encounters with revenants themselves, could not be swayed from their testimonies that the dead had indeed come back and were causing mayhem and much fear.

Calmet though, and Reverend Newburgh were not really describing the possibility that such creatures had been roused by the actual summoning of such revenants. In the medieval ages, Necromancy was often called 'Nigromancy,' meaning 'Black Magic,' and defined as "that which harms a person."

Rather than using magical ritual for healing purposes, the black art of Necromancy embraces the power of death and dying, that which cause decay and rot, and the powers that kill, and the Necromancer is attempting to harness these powers, called most simply 'Death Essence,' to use for their own sinister and dangerous purposes.

Seneca, the Roman Philosopher refers to Necromancy and Revenants as early as 4 B.C. The summoning ritual to create the revenant, he said, involved a sacrifice and knowledge of both the Moon phases and the position of Saturn to determine the best timing for conducting the ritual.

In ancient Egypt, Greece, Persia and Babylonia (an ancient Akkadian-speaking region and in Mesopotamia) and the earlier Chaldea region, Necromancy was recorded as prevalent, and practitioners were known as Nekromantia's or 'diviners of the dead.' Sometimes they were also called 'bone conjurers,' in the Hellenistic age. The book of Deuteronomy warns against such practice.

Necromancy is the blackest of all the dark arts. This ancient practise is a method of communing with the dead. It is the art of raising the dead and controlling them, controlling their spirits. It is the use of the spirits of the dead for divination or prophesy, as well as using them as slaves of the practitioner. It can be for used, for example, for channelling of a curse on an enemy.

In extreme cases, the corpse must be interred; it must literally be dug up from its grave, and its body is then used for grisly totems or talismans, which can be worn on the practitioner's body or used in his black magic rituals. Necromancy is the most dangerous of magickal workings, with very serious possibilities that the soul of the practitioner will never recover from his attempts at binding the spirit of the dead body to his own will. Tampering with and trying to use a deceased person's astral energies can be a battle and the will of the dead may overpower that of the black magician. The very soul of the practitioner may be fractured in the attempt, a fracture that will never recover.

In Thailand there is a rich tradition of Necromancy practitioners, and there are some who will make potent oils from bodies of the dead, using extractions of their bodily fluids and body fat, and selling them to those who are desperate or naive enough to purchase them at high prices. The dead body can be a useful tool for creating tinctures and oils and it is mixed with graveyard dirt, herbs, blood, and crushed human bone.

So terrible is the toll on the practitioner of necromancy according to 1800's French occult author Éliphas Lévi, that: "the experiences of theurgy and necromancy are always disastrous to those who indulge. No warning will save them. Weird sounds and sometimes bloody signs will appear spontaneously. They are always the same and are classed by magicians as diabolical writings. The very sight of them induces a state of ecstasy. These so-called spirits require sympathetic excitement. Catalepsy followed by madness,' he says, is usually the consequence.

Dante Abiel, a current day 'dark magician,' claims that in his pursuit of learning the art of necromancy he fell into insanity, lost 7 days of his life with no recall and 'came-to' in a graveyard, naked and covered in human blood. He claims he has no idea what happened to him during that period of 'lost' time, nor where the human blood came from.

He proceeded to write a book for those who wanted to learn necromancy, in which he offers the abilities to 'evoke the Gods of Death, eternally bind souls, Rituals for pulling spirits out of graves, how to open the Gates of Damnation through animal sacrifice, vampirism, and cannibalism,' and, 'the ultimate invocation of Death Essence...' All in all, something not to be tampered with lightly it is presumed.

The most notorious modern day alleged necromancer was perhaps British celebrity Jimmy Savile, who died in 2011. After death, he was accused of going to hospital morgues nightly to 'visit' with the dead. He had free roam of many hospitals due to his charity work, which raised millions of pounds for them. Testimony from many healthcare professionals after his death showed that some were well aware of his interest and visits to the morgues, although presumably they had no knowledge of necromancy. Grotesque and sickening reports were later given in official inquiries of "macabre accounts" of claims he had performed sex acts on dead bodies. Witnesses said he told them. Staff claimed he told them he interfered with patients' corpses, took photographs and stole dead patients' glass eyes to make into jewellery.

Jimmy Savile didn't need to inter the corpses; he had access to fresh ones, and from them he took trinkets and totems; he turned glass eyes into talismans and wore them in plain sight. What else he did while alone in the hospital morgues will never be known but the grotesque possibility exists that he used the dead bodies for more than his own professed sexual gratification; that he most likely used their bodies for the darkest of black magic; for necromancy.

He was the 7th son of a 7th son. In ancient folklore, the 7th son of a 7th son was from birth bestowed with 'magical powers, which could be used for good, or for evil. There is a strong historic belief that a 7th son of a 7th son in folklore would be a werewolf or vampire, fighting to keep his nature secret from the villagers, and roaming at night in his true form. The 7th son is often born with a natural gift for witchcraft, or wizardry. Their power in the occult is said to be great.

Saville himself said that people often said of him: "They were quite convinced I was a witch." And he added, "they'll say; "He's not what you think you know....the forces of darkness are at work there." He said it as a joke; but in hindsight, this was just one of the many clues he gave.

He was good friends with the Royal family, the Pope, Prime Ministers, and other politicians. It was even said that he worked for the British Secret Services, although of course, we don't know. He was a Freemason, Knight of Commander of St Gregory, and a Knight of Malta. Those were just the titles he had and the organizations he was known to publicly belong to....but perhaps there are others, not publicly known.

He said: "I am the 'Eminence Grise': the grey, shadowy figure in the background. The thing about me is I get things done and I work undercover." The phrase 'Eminence Grise' refers to a powerful decision-maker or advisor who operates behind the scenes, secretly in a non-public or unofficial capacity; a confidential agent, and one who exercises unsuspected power. They are machiavellian influencers. The phrase has been applied for example to Rasputin, the charismatic and mysterious mystical adviser in the court of Czar Nicholas II of Russia, who held the royals in his thrall, or to the Compte de Saint Germaine, a figure in history who appeared to be a key player behind instigating the French Revolution, a key figure in the founding of the illuminati, and an adviser to many European Kings, who gave him lodgings in their castles and set up Alchemy laboratories for him to use.

He was known to have been taught in the Mystery Schools of the Orient, and he would conduct his alchemical illumination rituals of ascended man in the laboratories of Kings. He, like Jimmie Savile, was a member of many of the Secret Societies. Savile had extraordinary exposure in the media, but it is behind the scenes that perhaps his greater influence lay. His 'powers' were like that of a Svengali-like figure. His persona would best be described as the Jester, for he was forever jovial and comical; although we know now he was really the

Trickster. He had an uncanny ability to influence, persuade, manipulate and control people.

He was a children's entertainer who said "Abracadabra" all of the time. Though the word Abracadabra may stem from an Aramaic phrase meaning, "I create as I speak," it is also widely associated with the occult. "Avada Kedavra" in the original Aramaic form meant; "Let the thing be destroyed," and at that time, it was intended for disease and plagues. It was said to have been used by the Gnostic sect of the Basilides to invoke benevolent spirits, and similarly by other Gnostics.

Aleister Crowley's "Abrahadabra" symbolized the accomplishment of the Great Work - The Magnum Opus within Thelema, as the process of attaining Knowledge and Conversation of the Holy Guardian Angel and learning and accomplishing one's True Will. The concept originates as far back as Medieval Alchemy and came to Thelema through Hermetic Magic and

Qabalah. "Abrahadabra" is 'The Key of the Rituals." In other words, it is believed by practitioners to be a word of astonishingly great power. He used the 'Mano Cornuto;' or the 'Horned Hand,' the symbol for the Pagan Horned God, interpreted often as a gesture made in satanic salute, and a demonstration of a sign of allegiance to other Satanists. It's an outward display of where one's affiliations lie; a sign of recognition between Lucifer's servants and an open declaration of allegiance to the dark lord.

A documentary by 'Society X' suggests it's highly likely that Savile was part of the order of the A. A. The A∴A∴ applies what it describes as 'mystical and magical methods of spiritual attainment' under the structure of the Qabalistic Tree of Life, and its aims are said to be the practice and teaching of 'Scientific Illunimism." Perfection of the individual on every etheric plane via a series of initiations is at its core.

Saville was a mixture of pied piper, trickster, and warlock. His outfits were garish, flamboyant and multi-coloured, just like a Harlequin, or a court Jester. 'Stanczyk' was the most famous Jester in the court of Poland. In paintings, despite and in contrast to his colourful attire, he is painted with a very concerned and reflective look on his face. Unlike other jesters of European courts, Stańczyk has been always considered to have been much more than a simple entertainer. He too was also called an 'Eminence Grise' and here perhaps we have the closest to the Harlequin character. Behind 'Stanczyk's cap n bells jester's costume was another powerful and cunning machiavellian influencer.

Says Dan; 'Cabalist magicians can create a revenant with human blood, corpses, or animal matter. A revenant is a magically created being. Similar to a golem. This is generally through ritualistic rites done at specific times. I know a lot about these practices because I spent my 20's playing in theurgy and thaumaturgy.'

Kabbalah author Colin Lowe writes: 'In medieval Europe the development of Kabbalah is believed to have been based on reinterpretation of documents from the near East such as Babylonia. Standard texts such as the Talmud were complimented by some very unusual texts that had been preserved in family lineages such The Sepher Yetzirah. These highly influential texts have a pronounced magical flavour. The Sepher Yetzirah in the medieval mind was literally a prescription for advanced magical practices culminating in the creation of life. Popular myth-making around this idea gave rise to the many stories about the golem, an artificial being made out of mud and animated by the power of Holy Names.'

The core essentials of any Necromancy ritual is said to be the conjuring of a Servitor, much like an elemental, or a 'thought-form' given shape and empowered with the Death Essence. It is the harvesting of Souls in its blackest form. Death encompasses far more than the physical death of the body, and the Death Essence or Spectral energy is released as the Life ends and a new cycle begins. The expert Necromancer is adept at harvesting that released death energy and manipulating it to meet his own ends.

Etheric Revenants, as coined by author John Michael Greer are believed to be very rare but very dangerous astral undead spirits, that feed on the energy of the living. Etheric Revenants are also the foundation of Vampire lore and the existence of such stems from the ancient Egyptian practice of preserving the body where in some cases it was believed the spirit may have the strength to maintain its etheric body through feeding off life-force rather than passing to death.

Vampire magic is said to be involved in Necromancy. Vampires, in the Bram Stoker form of course, do not exist; however, in Vampiric magic an expert necromancer will have honed his ability to use death to drain the life forces of the living. The drinking of blood is believed to drain life in ritualistic magick, and the fluids of a body too are said to be used by the practitioner in life-draining.

There is also the practise of 'Breathism' of absorbing the last dying breaths. A necromancer harnesses the Death energy of bodies. Energy cannot be destroyed. Death is another side of existence. Necromancers are capable of manipulating this death force of energy, like the life-force energy, and these death ethers are highly sought after by the adept Necromancer.

When the physical body ceases to function, one has experienced the First Death. When the etheric body weakens and finally loosens, believed to be within 24 to 48 hours, then one has experienced the Second Death. What the 'vampire' has learned to do is avoid the Second

Death by constructing what Greer calls an etheric revenant.

According to the Druid and Asatru adept who runs Monstersandmagic blog, in order for a 'vampire' to be created of themselves however, the person who dies would need to have the knowledge of how to create the etheric revenant, and while alive be adept in practice that will serve to strengthen their etheric body before physical death happens. Modern funereal methods of embalming and cremation destroy the ability to do this apparently, but if the body were wrapped as an Egyptian shroud, then the revenant could succeed if it were able to source supplies of etheric energy from the living to fed from. This 'feeding' of the vampiric revenant is said to cause serious degradation to the living it feeds from and can, it is said, result in death in those with weaker constitutions.

Druid Chris, host of the Hedge Druid blog describes a strange experience in a graveyard, when dowsing and communing with the Yew tree there. (Which may sound strange to us but is possible for those who are spiritually attuned it seems.) He 'heard' a message come to him from the tree, urging him to do something that 'might be dangerous, but worth it.'

He allowed his dowsing rods to lead him and came to a seat close beside some graves. He immediately began to feel weak, his energy draining from him rapidly and alarmingly.

Shortly, a new 'voice' began explaining to him that his energy was being taken by the entity that was now addressing him and the entity explained that it was not a living being but an entity which was a shroud or rather, the energetic remains of a living person. The 'remains' told him: 'visitors leave scraps of energy that we use to manifest.'

"I realised that of course, with the seat being there, people would be resting on it and thus providing this 'shade' with its meal-ticket. It was telling me that it had other knowledge and secrets to impart but I was feeling drained. It had done a good job on me whilst I was sat in the seat." He left as fast as possible, before he became too weak to leave.

Dan Mitchell thinks a revenant was unleashed upon the wife of a Reverend Pike. "She was being tormented and a mere demonic intrusion will not cause a person to jump off a bridge. This was something much more powerful. I will say that racing thoughts and dreams like the Pikes wrote about are classic symptoms of malefic entities. Hers was so much more powerful though. These were cabalistic magicians that were able to unleash a revenant against them, not a mere demon, a revenant. A human corpse or body is used as a vehicle for a particular discarnate intelligence, either a planetary intelligence of some sort, or the spirit of a dead person. Through various rites these corpses are animated and ordered to carry out some task. Ritual human sacrifice is done almost solely by cabalistic magicians that are always in the pursuit of power."

Reverend Ted Pike, who runs a national prayer network in the United States, has been vocal to his followers in the aftermath of a particularly difficult number of years in her personal life, which culminated in tragedy.

"It is with great reluctance that I reveal the bizarre circumstances that led to my wife's death." He was reluctant, he said, because, by revealing the circumstances, "I will almost certainly destroy my credibility with readers whose beliefs excludes the Supernatural."

It seems that it all began many years ago, and it began with him. In 1971, in his mid-twenties, after many years of Bible Study and comparative interpretations of the Bible, he decided to write an extremely controversial religious book, which would heavily criticize one particular religious group. Seeking solitude and quiet in which to write, he went off to a cabin in the Mountains. Shortly after this, strange things began to happen.

"I became very weak; so weak that I couldn't walk more than a few feet without needing to lay down. I began to experience visitations of what were very tangible presences in the night, which would temporarily paralyse me while overwhelming me with sensations of evil. This continued for more than a decade and I could only do light work for less than twenty minutes. If I persisted I would become so exhausted I would become immobilized for days at a time." His controversial book it seemed, was being prevented, by supernatural magickal means.

"My first, nearly finished 345-page manuscript was thrown into a wood stove and consumed. Another time I had seven pages of very important documentation for an article, stapled together. Page 5 disappeared."

His new wife, an artist "who used to walk ten miles a day and play the piano for hours a day, suddenly became extremely weak with inexplicable exhaustion. We tried to go on honeymoon, but we went barely a few kilometres before she became so sick and nauseous that she had to lie down beside the roadside."

Of course, one could suggest that this had to be a form of emotional contagion, and she fell under the impression of her new husband, her body mirroring his as he sunk into exhaustion. However, if she was somehow subconsciously copying him, she was even sharing his nightmares. "Once, while sleeping, I dreamt that an evil man was coming toward me, his hands about to strangle me. We awoke simultaneously. She said she'd had a nightmare, that an evil man was coming toward her neck, his hands out to strangle her."

Not long after marrying, they had gone out for a walk one late summer evening. His wife said there was an enormous black silhouette of a man's torso and head in the heavens. "As we left to go home, she said lights were appearing among the trees. After our walk, we both experienced presences, faces; the house was filled with presences. Sickening odours. Water dripped from dry ceilings. She saw an eye staring at her from inside the sink hole."

"She saw creatures like worms swarming around in the darkness. We heard scurrying. We heard banging. I saw tiny red lights in the house, in the trees. There were knocks on our doors but no one there. Human-like forms come in and out of our house. Our cats would flee from them. Garbled messages were left on our phone."

"Some will certainly say that what my wife experienced were hallucinations after she had brain surgery to remove a tumour. But she was not alone. I experienced it all too. Our house was filled with clicking sounds, streaking lights, whirring presences across the ceiling. They told her they were going to kill her and she didn't have a chance; they were too many. She saw glowing eyes staring at her out of the woods."

"Often, I would see tiny intense red lights in the trees and fields. She would frequently see human figures outside our house, including a man in a baseball cap, standing on the top of a fir tree. Once, she pointed out to what were large grass-green squares imposed like lattice on the forest. She said the entire sky was filled with poison oak leaves, every vein meticulously reproduced. She saw many strange apparitions in the sky, including scowling faces looking down on her."

Extraordinarily powerful magickal means, it seems, were entirely able to manipulate and alter the very landscape and all within it around them.

"On occasions she became entirely deranged, raving uncontrollably." One night she was lifted and thrown back and forth across a room. Another time she was thrown head first down a cliff. Somehow, she survived.

In 2011 his wife got in her car alone in the middle of the night, drove to Marquam Bridge, and jumped into Willamette River. "Did she commit suicide? No," says her husband. "Satan murdered her, throwing her off the bridge."

Many of his friends and family, though not wishing to believe in the power of magic, saw first-hand the unnatural forces that laid siege to his wife and himself.

The Reverend says: "Scripture tells us that Egyptian magicians had the ability to create living snakes. They created the most tangible physical reality. The anti-Christ's "image of the Beast" in Revelation will not just be a technological marvel; it will be satanically able to "breathe," "speak," and "put to death the saints."

Though the Reverend calls his wife's attackers Demons, Dan believes it was a revenant that drove his wife to throw herself off the bridge. 'It is clear they were being attacked by something malefic that was initially aimed at Ted. These were cabalistic magicians that were able to unleash a revenant against them, not a mere demon, a revenant. I have seen these things and they are very dangerous. It wouldn't surprise me in the least that Alynn's tumor was caused by them. I say this because these malefic entities exude radioactivity, this is why they are so dangerous.'

Reverend Pike says; "I believe bizarre occult phenomena such as crop circles, cattle mutilations, etc., are the work of the same. Every day for six years, my wife Alynn frequently babbled in tongues, and saying two names repeatedly. Students of Kabbalism will recognize these names. What she experienced were thought-control images emanating from an evil collective, coalesced into malevolent personalities. Alynn's demons were actually ghosts, i.e. departed souls, not fallen angels..."

But in Dan's case, and others, revenants can come fully manifest. The strange 'man' at the house Dan entered to find his friend: 'The sense I had of this person was that he was not human. Even though I refused to look at him, my mind's eye painted a portrait of a person not unlike the Harlequin. It was just wearing another disguise. He was very thin and wearing clothes that were too big for him. The voice was neither male nor female. It sounded androgynous. His skin was pale, his countenance was pallid. He seemed to be alive, but wasn't. He was some type of revenant and I could sense that he was very dangerous.'

'People who see revenants will describe them similar to the harlequin or as human beings that look fake, or wearing a mask.' Such as the incident in 1994 in which Dan and his friends saw "what appeared to be a young woman with blonde hair," when driving home from a party. "With every step she took, she became jerkier, her hair seemed to bounce more violently. The Harlequin was wearing a wig and pretending to be a "normal" person walking down the street. From the back seat someone said, "Oh my God her eyes!" A panic struck everyone.'

Karen Tooten of Postreason blog describes an incident that happened to her in the mid '70's. 'When I was 17 I was working in a small convenience store, (it was somewhat isolated) when a "woman" came in to buy cigarettes. At first I didn't pay any attention to her until I saw her hand (when she handed me the money) - it was not like a human hand. This startled me so I looked up and saw a very pale entity, wearing a thin black coat (like rain coat) with collar turned up to cover her neck, a heavy long-haired wig, and very large black glasses.'

'This did not entirely hide her strange face: a very pointed chin, scant lip and nose. She did not speak. Took her cigarettes and left! Oddly I cannot remember the details of her hand (though it was the first thing I noticed). Nor do I think she left in a car which was odd since most patrons drove up the store (it was isolated).'

'I wasn't paying much attention to her until I saw her hand. She was startlingly strange-looking. Other details that really jumped out at me like her hand, (were) her facial features were not human-looking. Whatever she was, the memory of her face has stuck with me to this day. But what I find really odd is that her hand - I cannot remember, the visual is completely gone.' 'As to the gender of the cigarette "lady" I have never been certain of that.'

Prior to this, as described in John Keel's Mothman Prophesies and indeed in the Saratosa

Journal, Mrs Shirley Cromartie, a part-time housekeeper at President Nixon's Key Biscayne residence insisted that after being arrested for shoplifting dresses, she had been hypnotised to do so by a strange woman wearing a wig.

She explained that upon arriving at the store parking lot, a strange woman approached her, asked her the time, and then ordered her to steal the dresses.

Said Mrs Cromartie: "I just sort of lost my will. It was a terrifying experience. Whatever that young woman did to me, it was like being in a sleepwalk, only awake."

She described the mysterious stranger as being attractive, young, and wearing a wig. When she raised one of her hands, this seemed to hypnotize the house-keeper, whose background was vouched for as being 'impeccable' by a senior figure in the FBI. A psychiatrist, on examining her said he believed her story as being truthful.

In Stratford, Ontario in the afternoon of April 25th 1978, ufologist Pat De La Franier was at his office going over some UFO sighting reports that he intended to present to a local UFO group when there was a knock at the door. Usually he could hear everyone coming in the main door, being admitted and then walking down the hall, but this knock came "from nowhere." When he opened the door, there was a very odd-looking man standing there dressed all in black, estimated to be about 5ft 6, and extremely thin. His head was slightly enlarged. His lips were very thin and his cheeks were "so sunken in that they looked like they were pinned on the inside. His eyes were dark and huge – they literally wrapped around his temples." La Franier stated that he had never seen eyes like that, and that "they just bored into me."

The stranger just stood there staring as La Franier felt as though he was being mentally "intruded upon." After this went on for what seemed at least a minute, the stranger then spoke: "Would you like a photograph of your family?"

The stranger's voice was very strange – it was faltering, "as if this man had no conception of how to speak or put a sentence together." When La Franier answered no, the stranger stepped backwards, turned and "just disappeared". Later La Franier would realize that many of his important files were gone.

Frank Taylor in his work The Uninvited, describes David Ellis and his wife Caroline who were landlords of a pub in Derbyshire in the early '80's, when they were called upon at just after dawn one morning. Two men in black, wearing matching suede gloves and who "looked like twins" arrived on their doorstep that early morning.

They insisted on entering, and as they did they removed their hats, where it was seen that they were both completely bald. What the couple most noticed however was that both men appeared to be wearing lipstick.

After this visit, the husband and wife started to receive weird telephone calls. They could not decipher who was calling them, but their voice was strangely metallic.

In another strange case, an English female health-care administrative assistant told ufoevidence organisation about her series of odd encounters. One evening in October 2014 at almost midnight, she was alone in her kitchen when the security light outside her home came on.

Concerned that it may be a fox trying to get at the chickens she kept in the garden, she got a torch and went outside to investigate. As she approached the chicken pen, she saw a figure standing to the side. She shone the torch in his direction and saw there were two figures standing there. They appeared to be men of extremely tall height, over six foot six she estimated. She shone the light at the closest figure's face. Immediately she heard a voice saying: "Please turn out the light."

She shone the torch into his face. "His face should have been there - but all I saw was a pointed mouth and glasses."

Both of them were now telling her to turn off the torch. She complied. "They asked if I had seen anything 'untoward.' They were using outdated phrases," she said, "like from the 1940's, and their accents were strange." As they turned to leave she noticed they had very long feet.

It happened again on another occasion, but at her workplace. "I was having a cigarette at work outside and using my phone when I saw the same feet in strange shoes. I looked up and I saw this thin pale gray face staring at me. This time as I watched him walk away he made no noise and I saw that he walked like he was made out of plastic. This scared me more than anything and I felt panic."

"I think I'm being watched now. I constantly catch glimpses of them in passing cars, in the windows opposite my office building."

Rev. Dr. R. W. Boeche is Pastor at Christ Lutheran Church, Lincoln, NE. Author and Founder of the Fortean Research Center. He has been involved in the study of unexplained phenomena since 1965. In his paper UFOs Caught in a Web of Deception, he interviewed a 29-year-old female insurance clerk 'SW' about her on-going strange encounters.

'After work I was walking to the lot where I park, and when I get toward my car this guy is next to my car. I figured he's trying to get into his car next to mine. But when I get closer, he doesn't look right. He was real tall and skinny, and he looked like... he was made of wax. Real pale and waxy looking. Like maybe he was dead or something. He was looking at me all the time, and he says to me: "Do not discuss your travels. It is not safe."

'Real sort of precise, but in a funny flat voice, no emotion. I got to the entrance of the lot, and looked back in my mirror - he was completely gone. There wasn't any way he could've got away from where I'd seen him in that little space of time!'

The interviewer, Dr. R. W. Boeche asks her: "When did the 2 dead-looking guys come to your door?"

"Somebody knocked at my door. There was the dead-looking guy from the parking lot, or at least somebody who looked a lot like him, and another guy who stood behind him - and looked like he could have been his brother. They both had that dead, waxy look."

"They said, "Your travels with the searchers. It would be unwise to discuss them with anyone." Then they kind of real jerky-like walk away, like some kind of wind-up walking doll that sort of rocks back and forth when it walks, real fast and jerky-like."

"I was so scared by the whole thing I broke down and cried. Spent the night in the living room with the lights on. I'm afraid they may show up again, and I don't know if I could take it. I'm afraid I'd just go crazy from it."

In 1968 in the town of Scarborough, Northern England, 16-year-old Adele was home alone. There was a knock at the door. Upon answering it, she was greeted by a tall man in a black suit and tie, who stood on the doorstep smiling widely at her for what she later described as an unnerving amount of time before he spoke.

He asked her if she had insurance. She replied that he should come another time when her parents would be home. The man appeared to then start sweating heavily, and speaking in what the girl described as "like a computerized voice."

He took off his hat and she saw that his head was bald and greatly contrasted with the colour of his face – then she realized, his face was caked in heavy make-up.He asked her if he could "see a glass of water." She took this as a request for a drink and she gestured for him to join her in the kitchen. As she handed the glass of water to him, he looked at it before placing it down on the table, and did not drink it.

He noticed the clock, and asked her about it, saying, "Is that your Father's time?" Confused once more, she answered that the clock had been a gift to her Father.

The man continued, "Is it here and now?" and began repeating the phrase over and over again. She said it was as though he was a robot that had begun to malfunction. He kept saying the same things, and his body was jerking, then seizing-up. She said that she noticed he found it difficult to move from the spot he was standing in and did so only with some difficulty, as though his legs had locked-up.

However, by the time he got to the end of the garden path, she noticed that he was now walking down the street at an ever increasing and quite alarming speed, almost, she said, at a superhuman speed.

'John' describes an incident, which was widely shared on forums when he told it a few years ago. It occurred when he was living in the center of a large City in the US. (He won't say which and is reluctant to identify himself, presumably because many will read his story with incredulity.)

'I would go for walks at night for years. I never felt afraid. But that changed one night. It was quiet, few people or traffic out. I went down a side street, and that's when I first noticed him. At the far end, on my side of the street; a man is dancing.'

'Thinking he was probably drunk, as I approached I gave him most of the sidewalk to pass by me. He was very tall and thin. His mouth was formed in an extremely wide smile. I crossed the street and looked back. He was facing me.'

'I started walking again, but kept my eyes on him. He didn't move.'

'I got almost a block between us. I looked back to where he'd been but he was gone. Then I saw him. He was in front of me. He started coming toward me. He was moving too quickly. His steps were giant.'

'Then he stopped, about the length of a car from me; with that smile.'

'After forever, he turned back slowly around and started dancing off. I watched him go until he was almost out of sight. And then I realized his shape was growing larger; he was coming back my way and he was running.'

'I ran. I ran until I was off that street onto a bigger street. I kept glancing over my shoulder, expecting to see that smile, but he wasn't there. I never again went for another night walk...'

In Italy in the winter of 1979 a night security watchman was on his usual patrol. A Mr. P. Zanfretta claimed that as he was filling his car with gas at a service station, he heard a voice calling him from the darkness nearby.

He claimed that he went toward the voice, almost as though compelled, as though he had no choice in the matter, and what confronted him was a tall human-looking being that had a large bald head, dressed in a suit, and wearing a grin that went from ear to ear.

Without moving his lips, this being spoke to him, compelling him to go back to his car, and drive it into a dark cloud that seemed to be hovering in front of him....

On her blog 'door without a key,' a lady called Steph writes of yet another encounter.'Years ago, my husband and I were driving around the county of Madera. It was quite a rugged area. We saw a man standing by the side of the road facing our way. He had a strange 'grin,' like he'd pulled his lips wide apart, yet I could see no sign of happiness. In fact, it felt confrontational.'

'We passed by. Traffic was very light on the road as we went on; we saw another car or so but weren't overtaken by anyone. As we drove on, we see facing us, standing beside the road again the same man with that same grin....'

In the district of Crosshill in the city of Glasgow, for three years women began reporting sightings of a 'demented,' and 'insane' figure which appeared in human shape and solid. Many of the women who encountered it were reportedly so traumatised and afraid that they moved from the area, to ensure that they would never encounter it again.

A woman in her fifties was woken one night by a strange snorting sound. Opening her eyes, she saw something at the end of the bed. It looked like a man, but from the light through the curtains she saw he was grinning at her in a maniacal fashion while bizarrely rubbing his hands fast up and down his chest. Screaming, she woke her husband up and he rushed to turn the light on. When the light came on, there was no-one there.

Two teenage girls were walking home late one night after a party. There was a near-full moon and so, although it was dark, they could see quite well. Suddenly they saw a man in front of them, whose appearance was decidedly odd. He looked perhaps to be in his fifties, they said. He was bald, and almost skeletal with an extremely thin frame. He was all in black. His movements were "jittery, as though he were incredibly agitated."

As they drew nearer, the hairs on the back of their necks stood up and they fell into terrified silence as they looked at him.

Walking as quickly as possible past him, they turned again to look at him and were stunned by the oddest expression on his face, which they described as being a "contorted combination between a grimace and an unnaturally wide grin." He was snorting and grunting at them.

They ran as fast as they could and when they looked back over their shoulders in fear that he would catch up with them, he had completely disappeared. There was no possible way, they said, that he could have gone so quickly out of sight, in just seconds - There was no-where for him to have gone, as the road behind them was wide and empty.

Anon says: 'The most intense and terrifying experience occurred during my college years.' Still living at home and commuting to college, this day she'd decided to stay in bed and try to grab some more sleep after her parents had left for work. 'As I was falling back to sleep, suddenly something changed. The room seemed charged with energy. It felt as if I were suffocating, as if tight bands were wrapped around my chest. I noticed a man standing in my doorway. He wore a red flannel plaid shirt with checkered print. He stood with his head thrust out, his eyes glaring up at me from under his brow. It was an extremely malevolent look, watching me intently. I was terrified. An understatement.'

'The Lumberjack Man' now stood closer to my bed, and he was grinning. I'll never forget that grin. Evil incarnate. When I was 8 I had a similar experience. I woke to see a man with black hair, a red plaid shirt, and his face was not normal, it was distorted with his mouth open and all kinds of crazy looking-teeth.'

Someone replies to her thread: 'This thread is freaking me out. It's almost exactly the same to an encounter I had as a child, in the early '70's. The only difference is that he wasn't wearing a check shirt... hard to describe. You know those plastic mannequin-like dummies they have in biology classes, where you can remove the various organs and stuff? That's what my "thing" looked like.'

'It started peeking at me from round my bedroom door. After seeing it a few times and trying to blink it away, I hid under the covers. When I peeked again, it was standing directly over me, looking down at me and smiling a toothy grin that was pure evil.' Another man wrote of his strange experience: 'A couple of years ago, my buddy and I decide to go for a drive. It's summer and hot and we were bored, so we get in his car and decide to drive up the mountain about an hour away from us. It's another hour's drive to get to the top of it and the roads are pretty precarious with tight bends.'

'It's pretty late, around 3 a.m. by the time we get to the mountain and start driving up it but we don't have to be up for work the next day. It's totally quiet, no other cars there and we're both really chilled. The road twists until you get to the peak so you can barely see round each corner and its pitch dark apart from some road lights. As we go round one of the bends I start to get this really weird uneasy feeling as I see something really strange. There's a person sitting on a boulder right at the edge. My friend's seen them too but carries on driving, and I'm thinking wtf but then I see he's turning the car round carefully and slowly and going to go back.'

'So we head back but I can tell he's still calm, not like me, so I tell myself it's just some crazy hiker. He stops the car dead beside the figure on the bolder and he shouts out to them, asking them if they're ok. I have to admit I'm pretty freaked so I keep quiet.'

'There's no response. Then the figure looks up and straight at us and we get the sh...t totally scared out of us. We see that it's a woman and she's wearing a long dress and she has beautiful long hair but it's her face; her face is like three times the length of a normal person's face and her eyes are completely empty; she's just staring at us blankly but she has this big creepy smile on her face.'

'I swear we both were so scared we couldn't move. We were completely frozen. We couldn't move, we couldn't say anything. I don't know how he managed to get his foot on the pedal and move the car and get us out of there, but i do know that when we got home, both of us were ill for quite a few days after that....'

An anonymous man writes: 'When I was about seven years old I was sleeping on the couch when there was a big storm. I got up to get a drink. A flash of lightning lit up the kitchen. I saw something; there was a figure. I see huge black eyes, his mouth is huge. His smile is much too large to be normal, I mean almost from ear to ear. I ran out. Needless to say, I couldn't sleep that night.'

'Then, about two years later my mom took my brother and I to meet her partner's parents. We got bored and asked if we could ride the bikes that were in the garage. We rode around on some trails. We raced each other on the trails, pedaling as fast as we could. Suddenly, I heard my brother screaming my name. I turned round and there was a truck just behind my back tire. The truck is really old and I see the driver and it's the same thing I saw in the kitchen; those teeth, and he was laughing.'

'I got off into the bushes and the truck sped off. My brother saw how big the mouth was - he told people about it; "that thing is not human; his whole mouth is his face....."

Chapter Seven:
The Ruse

Dan Mitchell

For a short time leading up to 2004, my life had become relatively quiet. My wife and I were preparing for the arrival of our first child together. In my spare time, I was still buried in my books and research. I began to study the classics of metaphysics and felt an affinity for the traditionalists. I had stopped with the eccentric and ritualistic type activities that had previously been a part of my personal practice. I began to look back at those activities with a degree of embarrassment. They felt somewhat undignified and even silly at times.

Even though I had witnessed strange things during these practices, and experienced peculiar and supposedly transcendent states of being, something was still missing. I had always believed that I was waiting for some type of enlightenment experience, and once it arrived, I wouldn't have to search any longer. I was in a state of constant inner change at this time. My ideas were always shifting and in a state of flux. I would build them up in order to destroy them by finding the points where they failed. This process revealed my own weaknesses and allowed me to understand the subtle mechanisms behind reality and the human mind. When I did experience those advertised states of being, the charm of them wore off rather quickly and a yearning still remained. I continued searching wherever I could and continued to be a highly conflicted individual.

My understanding of things around this time became much more reflective and philosophical. Just as I was changing and becoming more established and stabilized, inwardly and outwardly, the strangeness once again began to change.

In February 2004 my wife was eight months pregnant. One evening in the middle of the night we were awakened by a loud whirring noise coming from our bedroom. Although we were awake and alert, both of us were unable to open our eyes or move. It was a classic strike of paralysis. Suddenly, my wife saw a bright light come in through our second-story bedroom window. Since my head was turned away from the window, and I was practically looking into my pillow, I did not see this light.

During this event, I was receiving images in my mind of what appeared to be some type of creature that was either in the room with us, or just outside the window. It appeared to be a large, winged insect very similar in shape to a man. I felt threatened by this image, but since I was not able to physically see the source of the whirring noise, I did not know exactly what was happening. I only knew that I was awake and desperately trying to force myself to move my body.

As the noise began to fade out, I was finally able to move. My wife awoke out of the frozen state far quicker than I was able to. In a panicked voice she was calling for me to wake up. Initially, she thought that I had slept through the event. So many words began to pour out from her. She said she could see the room light up through her eyelids but was paralyzed. She was on the verge of tears and refused to go to the bathroom alone for the remainder of the pregnancy. Waking up in the middle of the night only brought us dread the first few nights after this had happened. Our biggest concern was if another abduction event was going to happen again.

She had no illusions about what had transpired that night. She understood that there was no reasonable or even scientific explanation for it. It just fit the profile. It was a failed alien abduction of some kind. She explained that she didn't know if she was being forced to remain still with her eyes closed by an alien presence, or if the paralytic state was caused by the fear of what was transpiring. This same paralyzing fear had been a staple of my childhood experiences of the paranormal.

When I finally came to and surveyed the bedroom that night, there was this hazy glow lingering in the air. Everything was exceedingly still. The residual glow slowly went away, and a fear began to set in for both of us. My wife explained that she was terrified that once she opened her eyes that she would see two bug-eyed, grey aliens standing in the bedroom. This was the imagery conveyed to her by the experience. She even worried that maybe our unborn child had been taken from us. This idea came from the UFO lore that had already been well-established in the culture. By 2004 there were dozens of televisions shows and moves that promoted the gray aliens, stolen pregnancies, alien examinations, and missing time.

Whatever happened that night marked a new development in the events that had been following me since childhood. Its new disguise came in the shape of UFO and alien abduction style events. This would turn out to be its most powerful disguise yet. From the time I was a child, UFOs had been a subject that deeply interested me. There was a profound mystique to the imagery and the idea of it all. It evoked a nostalgia in me emotionally. My brothers and I would lay in bed at night shining flash lights on the ceiling pretending they were the underside of UFOs.

About a week after this experience, my wife went to the public library and brought home a stack of books by Whitley Strieber for me to read. The experience was weighing heavily upon her, but she wasn't much of a reader. My grandfather had given me Strieber's book Communion to read when I was still young. Since I was only 12 when I first read it, I was too young to fully understand what was being conveyed. I knew that I was frightened by that book, but I also knew that I wanted to be a part of it in some way. I remember after reading Communion that I had attempted to set up "psychic contact" with aliens so that they might show themselves to me.

Reading through those books as an adult was an amazing experience because so much of Strieber's experiences matched things I had seen or felt. On Luminosity this was a common subject that I wrote about. Whitley Strieber read some of those posts even commenting once and linking to a review I did on his book, *Solving The Communion Enigma* in 2011.

Whitley Strieber's work is both unique and terrifying. Having engaged this phenomenon for many years, I understand him better now than I did years ago. I understand how people are changed by these experiences and how memories of the paranormal sometimes fade, get confused, or are added. I suspect that is because they are not entirely of this world. I understand the deep trauma they can inflict and how this trauma can function as the impetus to seek more meaningful answers. Unlike Whitley Strieber I do not view trauma as beneficial or evolutionary in nature. I believe quite the opposite. I believe that trauma is hard on both the body and mind. I believe it causes the personality to splinter and break and human bodies to break down due to stress. Trauma also causes people to cling too tightly to their ego and personal identity thereby mistaking criticisms as insults. This in itself only serves to magnify personal pain and suffering. For that reason I find his conclusions frighteningly sadistic and deeply flawed.

In reading Strieber's work I was reminded of Jaques Vallee's book, *Messengers Of Deception*. I saw subtle hints of duplicity in Strieber's narrative that bothered me. His writing functioned as a platform for the radical climate change cult that was attempting to win the hearts and minds of the masses. Their hypocritical prophets like like Leonardo DiCaprio and Al Gore told the world about their carbon sins, but it never stopped them from flying on private jets and leaving the lights on for weeks in their empty mansions. The same "spiritual" message was present in Communion and Strieber's other books. Essentially, he states that humans are a curse upon the planet. They are destroying themselves and the natural world out of personal greed and ambition. The aliens are here to offer us a new world because humans can't make one for themselves. The real question is who are the aliens exactly, or better yet, what group of people are they the fictional representations of? The alien mythos that were pushed in books and movies throughout the 1980s and 1990s had a lot of money, power, and influence behind it. It was a tool in the globalist war chest. President Reagan even got on board with the propaganda during his speech to the UN General Assembly:

"I occasionally think how quickly our differences worldwide would vanish if we were facing an alien threat from outside this world. And yet, I ask you, is not an alien force already among us? What could be more alien to the universal aspirations of our peoples than war and the threat of war?"

-Ronald Regan, September 21st, 1987

I do not deny that humans are greedy and ambitious, nor do I deny they are damaging the earth. I believe wholeheartedly in the sacredness of the natural world and in the deindustrialization of the planet. However, we are merely replacing cyanide with hemlock in believing that the forces behind the climate change push have the best interest of human beings in mind. Their ultimate goal is obvious: they want to rebuild the world with a new ambitious and greedy elite who will initiate the lower strata (i.e. poor people) into a soulless, rootless, cosmopolitan society in densely populated cities that are separated entirely from the actual nature they pretend to care for. This elite will exist as masters in a master-slave relationship. Once packed into the new "green cities," these poor souls will become worker drones in a social structure that incentivises non-participation in the rites of passage that were once a part of healthy human societies who were still connected to the natural world. The dark secret of this sinister process of resetting humanity, which is already well underway and nearing completion, is that many people must perish in order to make the vision possible.

The environmentalist-flavored messages from aliens that were so prevalent 30 years ago in UFO lore were merely a part of the process of initiating people into their new, state-sponsored mythos of progress via intercession by supernatural or extraterrestrial beings. Another aspect of the psychological indoctrination of the masses were television shows like *Ancient Aliens* that promoted the belief that various alien groups were the founders and builders of ancient human culture. The recent release of US military footage showing UFOs has validated people's belief in the existence of benevolent space aliens. That was always the plan. So few recognize the insidious and destructive nature of what is taking place.

I believe that Whitley Strieber had genuine encounters with beings that likely lived in the unseen domain. These experiences left a profound mark on him and the way he viewed the world. His visitors may have been attracted to him for his creativity and ability to express the strange nature of what was happening to him.   For me, any discussion of aliens, abductions, and encounters with ambiguous entities must include his literary corpus. He wrote the book.   It was Whitley Strieber that brought these types of stories to the forefront of modern culture.   The real question is what is really hiding in his closet?   How did genuine high-strangeness encounters suddenly transform into spiritual propaganda designed to deceive people? That is a question for another time.

After our son was born, I began to notice that he had a guardian keeping watch over him every night for months. This guardian came in the form of a large owl that was perched on the power lines across the street only forty feet away from our son's bedroom window. If he woke up crying at night, I would come in his room and always see the owl looking directly at me through the window. It had deeply bothered my wife and me. Since my wife was not familiar with deeper alien abduction lore outside of stolen pregnancies, she was blissfully unaware of the link between owls and aliens. It was something I kept quiet about.

Around this time there were more troubling developments. I had been working 2nd shift for a time so my wife would usually leave dinner out for me when I got home. One evening I fell asleep while sitting on the couch after eating dinner. Something suddenly woke me up. As I looked at the wall in front of me I saw movement. I saw what appeared to be a creature scurrying up the wall. It looked like a spider-jellyfish hybrid. I quickly grabbed the steak knife that was on the plate next to me and threw it at the wall while letting out a muffled shout. I was horrified by its appearance and the way it moved. As I looked at it, it sort of phased out like it had noticed I was looking directly at it. I cannot stress enough the grotesqueness of how this creature moved.

As it crawled up the wall, it dragged these long, dangling dead legs behind it. Its body was translucent and jelly-like but it had a perceivable dark outline. I would later learn that these creatures are literally everywhere in our physical world, just hidden from our sight. They come in various shapes and sizes and are often attached to people's bodies in a parasitical fashion. My ability to see it that night likely stemmed from waking up too quickly. The creature was unable to phase out quick enough so my physical eyes caught a brief glimpse. One thing was certain, it was aware that I had seen it. Despite it being no longer visible, I could still sense its presence in the room.

Around this time I began to seek guidance and advice. I networked with others enduring similar experiences. Most of them were heavily into new age ideas and were deeply immersed in the alien abduction lore. I witnessed quite a few of them suffering from mental and physical ailments. They used terminology and phrases that belonged to other authors and experiencers. I was looking for something more personal, something that came from deep within others who experienced these things. The people I wrote to were convinced that they were walk-ins or that their souls had come from another galaxy. They all professed a belief that they were originally divine, and that their sojourn on earth was a learning experience of some kind. Aliens were either helping them along or thwarting their progress. They could never explain why, if they were previously divine, that they had to come down to earth to begin with. The fact that so many people I communicated with were immersed in the UFO and alien abduction lore made it difficult to know where their personal stories began and where the Strieber-Hopkins narratives ended. I was just out of my element entirely.

I eventually burned a lot of bridges when I began to question and challenge their ideas about what was really happening to them. In my mind they were too easily convinced by the various narratives floating around. Sometimes even the most explainable phenomenon got blown up to monumental proportions. An out-of-place cigarette butt found on a porch suddenly meant that a soft-spoken housewife was being stalked and targeted by government agents. A man who always looked at the clock at 11:11 somehow knew that this meant he was a life-long abductee who had a mission to save millions of people from a cataclysm that was due to strike in 2010. The problem that I always saw in these stories was that they came from people who buried themselves in paranormal lore to the point that every anomalous event they experienced was filtered through the narratives they had read or the sacred cows they bowed down to. Ultimately, their stories lost their own meaning and purpose in the weltanschauung of other well-known writers and con-artists. I did not want that to happen to me.

In the fall of 2005, my wife and I had our second child together. I continued to delve deeper into my early childhood experiences. I began to once again obsess over missing person cases as I always did. Seeing pictures of the missing had always caused a kind of psychic explosion to go off inside of my head. Looking into their eyes, I knew that many of them no longer walked among the living but didn't quite seem dead either. I noticed in many of the cases a gradual breaking away from reality before the victims simply vanished leaving behind nothing more but an eerie story that evoked a stifled fear in people. I saw a link that I couldn't quite define between the events I had been experiencing and missing people. This would lead me down many dark roads that I am still investigating to this day.

I was still meeting with my mom and asking her questions about certain times where it felt that something strange may have happened. When I made attempts to speak with my dad about his memories, the communication was always brief. He simply did not want to engage. He has always known much more than he was willing to talk about.

I began to ask my brothers questions about our childhood as well. One of them remembered nearly as much as I did. We shared stories of confrontations with homeless people who had chased us around the neighborhood while we screamed in terror because the homeless people seemed un-human. He remembered seeing very small children standing on branches high in the tree just outside our bedroom window. Though we all used to climb that tree along with our friends, the heights he saw these kids at was impossible. Like me he remembered sitting in the back seat of our parent's car when my oldest brother was sucked out of the window. He always thought that was a fever dream but I remembered it as well and the fear of never seeing my oldest brother again. I had to ask myself honest questions. Was I having dreams that were so vivid that I had merely mistook them for real events? Are shared dreams even real? My brother and I shared so many of these odd memories with only the slightest differences.

As extraordinary and outlandish as the memories were, I began to believe in them. I began to piece together a story so incredible that there was no way to reasonably present it to people. For many years I just sat on these memories while we endured more manifestations of UFOs and otherworldly communications in the form of powerful synchronicities. Seeing UFOs had become commonplace for my wife and me. It felt as though whatever was in the sky or in our house was performing for us. I noticed the theatrics of the phenomenon in general. The Harlequin itself was theatrical. Even life itself at times seemed theatrical.

In 2007 I had what I would call the most pronounced UFO encounter I had ever had. At some point during the night someone frantically began to ring my doorbell. When I opened the door there was a young woman standing there. I knew her well. Years earlier I made a decision that would impact her life and hurt her a great deal. While this transpired I saw that we were being observed. Just down the street hovering in the air I saw an enormous object in the sky. This thing would have rivalled the size of what I witnessed during the event in 1984. It was easily the size of a skyscraper and was intimidating to look at. I distinctly remember having a difficult time looking up. Even though it was dark, I could see the outline clearly in the sky. I couldn't look at it for long without feeling as though I would be pulled up and taken away by it. I felt powerless.

I could tell that she was frightened. Being nearly a thousand miles away from home she had no clue where she was. As I stepped outside I could see in her eyes that she recognized me. I did my best to comfort her while also apologizing and encouraging her that everything would be fine. She didn't say anything. As this was happening I was receiving intuitive instructions that I ignored with every fiber of my being. I was told that my "best option" was to leave my life behind and go with this woman onto the ship that was hovering down the street. How could I do that?

After saying "no" to what was coming across my intuitive sense, I explained to her that she would have to go back with the "people" that had brought her to my door. This distressed her greatly. I remember walking her a short way toward the hovering object and then feeling the presence of a person, whose face I could not see, take her away.

My memory of this event is as real as any memory that I have. Though I was in an altered state of consciousness, there was realness to it. However, like I mentioned earlier, the experience lacked continuity. I have no solid memory of approaching the door or returning to the house after she was gone. I just woke up the following morning with the memory strongly in my mind along with the associated emotions the experience evoked in me.

These are things that I have been unable to forget or dismiss as artifacts of an overactive imagination. Luminosity had a modestly sized audience. The attention it received seemed to be enough to add fuel to a phenomenon that was already affecting me in negative ways. Everything that had happened to us before 2010 would pale in comparison to what happened when I began to write about these matters publicly. Not only did I gain the attention of abductees and spiritual seekers of all kinds, I also got the attention of military contractors, naval intelligence, DHS, and FBI. All of these and more became regular visitors to my blog. Many of them even wrote to me personally about the material I was producing.

I did not just write that blog, I lived every terrible moment of it. I created it to document my experiences and the experiences of my family in real time. What started out as a genuine attempt to make sense of things spiralled into pure insanity and earned me a bad reputation. That was solely on me.

The entity behind the phenomenon I experienced was not a kindly forest sprite, ghost, or extraterrestrial dedicated to saving the planet and the human race. It belongs to the realm of the unknown which cannot be picked apart by reason or logic. It shows up when it wills and departs when it wills. It is bound to people that in some way are able to express its mystique. I don't believe these are harmless creatures. They aren't! There is a danger in communion with beings who don't live by the same rules and laws of nature that we do. People have lost their minds, died, or have vanished from the face of the earth. Monitus es!

Conclusion

The threat to Dan and so many others,
continues in Book 2.

~ ~ ~ ~ ~

If you enjoyed this book, please be kind enough
to consider leaving a Review on Amazon.

Thank you.

Dan Mitchell can be reached at:
Danm1976@protonmail.com

Dan & Steph Young can be heard on the Podcast
Tales of Mystery Unexplained

Steph's other Books
https://www.amazon.com/Steph-
Young/e/B00KE8B6B0

UK https://www.amazon.co.uk/Steph-
Young/e/B00KE8B6B0/

Steph can be reached at:
Stephyoungauthor@gmail.com

Printed in Great Britain
by Amazon